A Poet in the House
PATRICK
KAVANAGH
at Priory Grove

We drift and we care not whither,
Why should we care?
For You are at the end of all journeys
By vision or prayer.

Blow us O wind, O blow us
Whither you will.
Every leaf that November casts clay-ward
Shall its own place fill.

Patrick Kavanagh, 'Drifting Leaves'

A Poet in the House
PATRICK KAVANAGH
at Priory Grove

Elizabeth O'Toole
Edited by **Brian Lynch**

THE LILLIPUT PRESS
DUBLIN

First published 2022 by
THE LILLIPUT PRESS
62–63 Sitric Road, Arbour Hill
Dublin 7, Ireland
www.lilliputpress.ie

A CIP record for this title is available
from the British Library.

Paperback ISBN 9781843518242

10 9 8 7 6 5 4 3 2

Set in 12.5 pt on 17 pt Perpetua by iota (iota-books.ie)
Printed in Kerry, Ireland, by Walsh Colour Print

An Chomhairle Oidhreachta
The Heritage Council

This publication is supported
by The Heritage Council.

patrickkavanaghcentre.com

Comhairle Contae Mhuineacháin
Monaghan County Council

The Lilliput Press gratefully acknowledges the financial
support of the Arts Council / An Chomhairle Ealaíon.

Contents

Illustrations between pages 88 and 89.

Editor's Preliminary Note

The many questions raised by the memoir about the precise dating of the events it describes, beginning with the first sentence, are discussed in the Afterword.

Preface

BRIAN LYNCH

Elizabeth O'Toole's memoir, which she completed in 2019 at the age of ninety-five, was written in the United States, where she has lived much of her adult life. Distance from her native country is just one of many reasons why she is not mentioned in any of the Patrick Kavanagh biographies; and it explains, too, why very few people, perhaps only historians of the Irish theatre, will remember that her husband, James Davitt Bermingham O'Toole, had once been a controversial playwright in Dublin.

Elizabeth was born in County Clare in 1924. Her father, Laurence Ryan, was a thoroughbred horse breeder; her mother, May Watson, was from Charleville, County Cork. Elizabeth was educated at Laurel Hill secondary school in Limerick, and at Cathal Brugha Street College in Dublin, graduating with degrees in Nutritional Science and Home Economics Education. Before her marriage, in 1948, she taught in County Cork, and, after moving back to Dublin, she was a lecturer at the Church of Ireland College of Education, at technical schools in Dundrum and Ballsbridge, and at her alma mater, Cathal Brugha Street College.

Jim O'Toole's background is exotic. He was born and brought up in Shanghai, where he had a brilliant career as a student, but the violence preceding the war between China and Japan forced his family to leave the city in 1934. By 1938, however, he had two degrees from University College Dublin, in engineering and geology. In February 1939, almost immediately after graduating, he went to Berlin to work for the Siemens company. There, he went into hiding from the Nazis, and managed to escape back to Ireland only at the beginning of January 1940.

The O'Tooles had been friendly with Patrick Kavanagh at least since the early 1950s – Elizabeth had been in contact with him when she was a student in Dublin in the early 1940s. They had four children and were living in the rapidly expanding suburb of Stillorgan by the time the poet came to live with them for about six months in 1961. As the memoir and the invaluable photographs show, the family were very fond of him.

Elizabeth O'Toole's daughter, Margot, adds a chapter, 'Patrick Kavanagh at Priory Grove'. As well as recording her own memories of Kavanagh, her contribution also contains significant information about her father's time in Berlin at the outbreak of World War II. This is followed by a very brief evocation by her mother of growing up in County Clare. Finally, some of the questions raised by all these memories and their literary and historical background are considered in an Afterword.

But the voice the reader hears most clearly is that of Elizabeth O'Toole. She speaks for herself, and what she says in 'A Poet in the House' both deepens, changes and challenges the way we see Patrick Kavanagh.

A Poet in the House

Elizabeth O'Toole

It was a winter night after Christmas. There had been a relentless downpour of sleet and rain all day. It was bitterly cold, chilling to the bone. Hearing our car, I ran out to welcome my husband, Jimmy. In the half-dark I nearly fell over a sack on the doorstep. I bent down to pick it up. It was soaking wet, and it wasn't a sack at all. It was Patrick Kavanagh.

'I couldn't take him to his flat: it's too cold and he's in bad shape. We must get him a hot drink and dry clothes,' Jimmy said as we helped Paddy to his feet and brought him into our house in Priory Grove, in the Dublin suburb of Stillorgan. Kavanagh coughed and spat up on the back of his hand a bright red foam. There was a smell of blood.

'Hospital,' I cried in alarm. 'Get him to a hospital at once.'

'No, no, no! I don't want a hospital. Please,' he pleaded, reaching out his arms.

'Paddy,' I whispered, 'you're very ill.'

'Yes.' I could hardly hear him.

My children, Margot, Larry and EllyMay, had come out into the hall.

'Mama,' Margot said, 'it's daddy's friend.'

'We'll do whatever you want, Paddy. We'll put you to bed,' Jimmy said as he swept him up in his arms and started carrying him up the stairs, calling to our son, 'Larry, help me here.'

I blocked the stairs.

'This man needs a doctor,' I insisted. 'Take him to a hospital.'

'Please!' Paddy said. 'I don't want to die in a hospital.'

'Nobody is talking about dying,' I said. 'Don't you dare die on me.' But I stepped aside, and Jimmy and Larry proceeded to half-carry Paddy up the stairs.

Margot squeezed past her dad, switched on the light in our bedroom, and turned back the bedclothes.

'Mama, he's all wet,' Larry called to me as he and his father were pulling off Paddy's clothes. I was in the bathroom filling a bucket with water.

'A hot bath would be great,' I said, 'but I think he's too weak. Jimmy, ring Paddy's doctor, ask him what to do, and get him to come as quick as he can. Larry, here are some towels. Use them to rub him all over to help his circulation, and then put your dad's pyjamas on him. Margot, let his feet warm up in this bucket. I'll fill some hot-water bottles and take his temperature.'

'Will Paddy be all right?' asked EllyMay.

'Yes, but we need to take good care of him.'

'And say prayers?' she asked.

'Yes, prayers. You're the best to say prayers.'

And that is how Paddy Kavanagh came to our home.

Later Jimmy told me that he had parked his old Riley car at the corner of Baggot Street and Stephen's Green in the centre of the city, and, when he had got back to it to drive home, he had found Paddy draped over the bonnet. Paddy had realized he was too sick to be able to make it home to his own flat; recognizing the car, he had decided his best option was to wait there because he knew Jim would take care of him.

The doctor came and agreed that Paddy should be in hospital, but he was now warm in bed and wanted to stay where he was. He was so dead set against hospital that the doctor thought it best not to stress him any further. He had the flu and a high fever. The worry was pneumonia.

'Let's hope for the best,' the doctor said. 'Keep him warm and quiet. Plenty of drinks, and a good sleep can work wonders. I'll stay in touch. Maybe Jim can sit with him tonight?'

So we tip-toed around and spoke in whispers. I knew Paddy needed nursing, and I did the best I could. I put a fire on in the bedroom, propped him up on pillows, and spoon-fed him with chicken broth, beef-tea, and hot lemon honey drinks. After a while, his fever broke.

When the danger of contracting the flu from him had passed, Larry or Margot sat with Paddy over the next few days and reported if he was grumbling, grunting, groaning, sleeping, or snoring. Margot even did her homework in his room. He was still not strong enough to get out of bed on his own, so Larry or Jimmy would take him to the bathroom. He was depressed. Jimmy read to him – sometimes just the headlines of the newspapers.

One morning Jimmy came down and said, 'He's very low today. Can you sit with him a while? The doctor said he'll come this morning.'

I went up to Paddy. I fluffed up his pillows, sat him up, told him he was looking much better and that he should have patience and let time be the healer. Then I sat on the end of his bed and decided against small talk. I relaxed and tried not to feel awkward, for I knew he was staring at me.

After some time, he said, 'I trained a woman in London once to sit on the end of my bed all night, like a dog.'

I answered in measured tones, 'Anyone who can dish out guff like that hasn't much wrong with them.'

As I bounced out of the room, I heard a scart of a laugh from Paddy. This I understood because, in the days before we had television to entertain us, a man, or indeed a woman, might sometimes make an outrageous remark just to knock a rise out of someone and start a contest of words.

'How is he?' the doctor asked.

'There's no fear of him,' I replied. He laughed figuring, based on my tone, that Paddy had said something to ruffle my feathers.

The dark rainy days of winter were rolling by. Paddy was steadily improving. Jimmy took him up a fine bowl of porridge in the mornings. He got scrambled eggs or a chicken sandwich for lunch, shepherd's pie or something like it for supper. Jim and myself were still sleeping on the mattress we had thrown on the floor of the girls' room the night Paddy arrived. I had thought that he would be up and gone soon.

My youngest child, Jacqueline (Jaja), had taken to having a nap in the mornings. So having waved the other three children off to school and my husband to work, with Paddy fed and Jaja asleep, I'd sit down in the kitchen, pour myself a cup of tea, watch the morning sun light up the marmalade on my toast, rest my arms on the old oak table, close my eyes and try to recapture some of the night's lost rest.

One morning an unmercifully loud racket jump-started me back to life. It was Paddy, banging on the floor and shouting, 'Woman, where are you? What's going on down there?'

'There's nothing going on,' I said. 'And my name is not Woman.'

'I want my breakfast.'

'You got your breakfast. Jimmy took it up to you.'

'My juices weren't up then, so I couldn't eat it. Now it's gone cold.'

'That's too bad. Eat it cold. It's just as nutritious.'

What a child, I thought. Just then Jaja began to cry.

'Paddy,' I said a little more calmly, 'you've woken Jaja. Why don't you come down and make your own breakfast?'

'I can't. You've taken away my clothes. What have you done with them?'

'I threw them out.'

'You threw out my clothes!' There was a shocked silence. 'God damn it, woman, you can't throw out a man's clothes.'

'They were worn out, falling apart, soaking wet.'

7

I rummaged through the drawers and found some of my husband's underwear, a pair of old tweed trousers, a flannel shirt, and a gansey. I laid them on the bed.

'I'll heat up your breakfast this time,' I said, 'but in future eat it when you get it. You're not at the Ritz, and I have work to do.'

And Paddy did get up and started to potter about the house, making a general nuisance of himself. He was gruff, but to me his gruffness was a good sign. It was an improvement over how depressed and lethargic he had been when he'd arrived. I lit a fire in the living-room. I thought to myself that Paddy could sit there and read and write or listen to the radio. I could live with that. I went about my life and tried to ignore my obstreperous housemate.

When a day turned up fine and breezy, I set about doing a family wash. My washing machine was an old model that required the washed clothes to be put through an electric wringer before being hung out on the line to dry. Paddy appeared in the kitchen.

'I want you inside. I want to read you something I have written.'

'Paddy, I'm busy.'

'I don't want you busy. Come by the fire and listen to this.'

'Not just now. I can't.'

'You're out here working like a whore. Come by the fire and listen.'

'Just as soon as I have these hung out.'

Paddy picked up the box of clothes pegs and went out into the garden. I hurried after him. As I arranged the clothes on the line, he pegged them down. After a while he said, 'I used to do this for my mother.' He was resting his hand on the line and tears were falling down his face. I could see that he was overcome by gentle memories.

'Thank you,' I said. 'Now I can listen. Let's go in.'

I sat by the fire, and Paddy began to pace, reading from his freshly written piece, stopping now and then to look at my face, to change a word, or to go back to his first thoughts. I was interested, and I was flattered. The great Patrick Kavanagh – a man whose poetry I had loved ever since I had first read it as a student at Laurel Hill secondary school in Limerick, was treating me like an equal, seeming to ask my advice.[1] Life was good. I stretched my legs towards the fire. However, I made the mistake of asking a question.

'Woman, I want to talk to you, and I want you to listen, but I don't want to have to educate you first.'

'Paddy,' I said, 'I'll listen to you, but I don't want to have to put manners on you first. I need to know what you're talking about, so don't think you can get up on your high horse with me.'

'Just listen. I have sisters and they let no one get a word in edgeways.'

'I'm sure they're bright. Why should they just listen and not ask a question if they have one?'

But then I caught myself. Paddy was focused on trying to write. Why hassle him? He was not seeking my input on the 'battle of the sexes' or any other run-of-the-mill subject unrelated to his poetry. Changing my tune, I said gently, 'You were about to read to me.'

Immediately he changed. His irritability had fallen away.

'We're not having an exchange of opinions,' he said. 'This is different. Have you ever listened to a stream? Well, of course you have. The water is the water, and what you hear as it comes down the hill is the sound it makes when it bounces off the stones in the stream. I want you to be like the stones – silent. Let the words go where they may.'

'Or I could be the trees with the breeze whistling through them.'

'Yes,' he said, elated. 'Nature makes music and poetry all day. All we have to do is listen. Now listen and be silent. Hear the songs of your secret self.'

He picked up his papers and continued to read, and sometimes to re-read, what he had written. I began to understand that much of his grumpiness was caused when his train of thought was disrupted. His voice was the instrument that made the sounds, but he had to be bouncing them off someone, and this time it was me. Poetry, he explained, had to be read aloud. You didn't get it if you were just reading it silently to yourself. As I embraced my role as Paddy's silent listener, the house became a little more disorganized each day. Throwing in a bit of understanding, Paddy started following me as I took the clothes from the line, made the beds, swept the floor, and prepared the meals.

During the months we spent together in the mornings, with the children off at school, Paddy talked to me about whatever crossed his mind – his younger brother Peter, and how they had shared a flat in Dublin, a very pleasant time while Peter was in college. He talked about being with his sisters and their friends as he helped with making hay and building ricks of straw. He talked about how visiting his relatives reminded him of Dylan Thomas's description of visits to his aunt in Wales. He gave me his perspective on specific events from his past. And, of course, he talked about his mother. Just as he had asked, I remained silent as stones and let his words bounce off me. It dawned on me that I was being presented with an unanticipated and serendipitous opportunity. I was getting to know and understand Patrick Kavanagh. Much has been written about Paddy and his poetry by scholars and poetry lovers. I have now decided to share my experiences of the exceptional person who left this treasured literary legacy to us.

Before his time as my truculent housemate, I knew Paddy as Jimmy's friend, and this famously irascible man had already made an impression on me. As has been previously widely described, Paddy was often followed around by an entourage of admirers and 'hangers-on'. Sometimes he arrived at our house in the company of such people. Once, a journalist needled him for having worn old clothes to the wedding of the movie actress Kathleen Ryan and Dr Dermod Devane.[2] The reporter 'supposed' that Paddy considered himself above having to conform to the conventions of dressing appropriately for such a high society affair. I was uncomfortable that Paddy, a guest in my home, was being derided in such a way over a trivial matter involving an event that had occurred years previously. But Paddy, seemingly accustomed to having to suffer this type of socially aggressive and gratuitous affront, did not bristle, as I believe most people would have. He replied with a mild statement of fact: 'I wore the best clothes I had.' Much of what has been written and said about Paddy describes him as a rude and difficult person. These descriptions always make me wonder about how many personal insults Paddy bore on his way to obtaining his reputation for irascibility.

I also memorably crossed paths with Paddy on the night Jimmy's play, *Man Alive!*, opened at the Olympia Theatre, in January 1961. The venue was sold out, and everyone who was anyone was there. The air bustled with excitement. I was standing in the wings with Jimmy and Jim Fitzgerald, the director and producer, as they named the stream of people taking their seats. Jimmy was delighted when he saw Paddy taking his seat. They went on to identify Erskine Childers and Patrick Hillery (both future Presidents of Ireland), the actor Godfrey Quigley, the poet and critic John Jordan and the playwright Brendan Behan, among many others.[3]

At the intermission, as I stood with Larry and Margot, Paddy came up to me. I was a little apprehensive, for he was well known for 'let-'em-rip' criticisms.

'Paddy!' I said. 'I'm so glad you could come.'

'I'm so glad I didn't miss it. It's a great play, some wonderful lines. Don't let anything you read in tomorrow's reviews upset you. Likely they won't praise it, or, worse yet, they'll damn it with faint praise and condescension. But don't let it get you down. A play like this, that is torn out of the blood and guts of life, is just too much for them.'

When the curtain came down to the thunderous applause, Paddy Kavanagh stood up in one of the front rows, turned to face the audience and said, 'Remember this applause when you read the reviews in the morning. Newspapers are lily-livered.'

Paddy was partly right. *Man Alive!* received mixed reviews. For example, John Jordan gave it a wonderful and perceptive write-up in *Hibernia* magazine, but the reviewer for *The Furrow* (a Catholic journal) slammed it.

After he had been with us at Priory Grove for a few weeks, Jimmy brought some of Paddy's clothes from his flat, as well as his typewriter and his mail. The clothes were old, but Jimmy said they were the best he could find. He hadn't bothered to take any of his socks because they were all full of holes. Paddy had also asked Jim to bring his cobbler's last and his toolbox. Great, I thought, he's going to set up shop here and never leave.

March roared in and life began to return to normal. 'Normal' meaning that I'd mastered the art of putting up with things and being somewhat gracious about it. At my invitation, Paddy moved his typewriter down to the dining room table. Next came his last, his hammer, nails and mugs of nails, tacks and screws – and all the 'gear and tackle and trim' as Gerard Manley Hopkins describes in 'Pied Beauty'. Paddy walked around from room to room before deciding to use one end of my kitchen table for his cobbling work. He put two new heels on his boots, and he built up the worn heel on one of Larry's shoes. Then he cleared a shelf for books and papers in the front room and seemed happy enough, whistling to himself now and then.

One Saturday morning Paddy was up early and trying to get the ribbon running in the typewriter. He was muttering and cursing. Margot went up to help. They soon got it working. Downstairs I heard the clicking of the keys again. But when Margot was looking over his shoulder, she saw that he had incorrectly spelled a word.

'Oh shit,' Paddy said. 'It doesn't matter.' And he kept banging away.

After a while Margot told him that sentences had to start with a capital letter.

'I don't give a curse,' he said. 'Find me a long business envelope. Do you know where your father keeps them?'

Margot went downstairs and returned with an envelope.

'Now,' Paddy said, 'I want you to do something for me. Your father is going downtown. Go with him. He'll take you to the office of the *Farmers Journal*. You go in and ask for the editor. His name is there on the envelope. When you meet him, tell him you have an article from Patrick Kavanagh and that he wants five pounds for it. Hold the letter tight in your hand and don't let go until you have the money in your other hand. Then say, "Thank you, sir," and leave immediately. That's important. Don't wait for him to open the envelope. Walk smartly out with your head in the air. Your father will be waiting outside. That's how business is done.'

The strange thing is the plan worked.

'Mama!' Margot said when she got home. 'At school we have to use the right spelling. But Paddy makes money writing and he spells words wrong.'

'Well,' I said, 'life can be a puzzle. Paddy and your dad are two big puzzles for me.'

Some time later the editor of the *Farmers Journal* told Jimmy that Paddy had offered him a deal: if the *Journal* took four or five such articles, he would send in 'the most wondrous article' for free – but he had to get his money first. By the time the 'wondrous article' was submitted, Paddy had already received £25 to £30 for the 'free article'.

Toward the end of March, Paddy received a letter from University College Dublin, reminding him that he was scheduled to give a lecture.

'You see, Betty,' he sighed, 'they gave me the job when they expected me to die. They didn't want it said that I died without recognition and with not a penny to my name, like Raftery the poet.[4] They wanted me buried as Dr Patrick Kavanagh, Professor of Poetry. But God pulled a fast one on them, and I didn't die. I got the lectureship, but really it's not what I want. I didn't ask for it, and I have no time for it. It takes away from what I should be doing. But I couldn't turn it down. It was good of them to give it to me, but I am no good at it. I have all these young people asking me questions about how to become a poet, and how do you know if you are one. I can't answer them in any way. I would if I could, but it's not my thing. I can't even settle down to prepare a class. Also, they want to know why I have given up my religion. But I haven't given up my religion. I have nothing against my religion, but I don't want to talk about it. I have given a few lectures, if you could call them that. It's really hard to be there with all these young people expecting some brilliant pronouncement. Your Jimmy could deal with that; his mind is quick. My mind is busy at something else; I have no gift for answers. But I need the cheque. It's not much, but it tides me over.'

'Paddy,' I said, 'if you've given a few lectures, you've more than earned your pay. Jimmy will collect your cheque. He can explain that you're recovering from pneumonia and that you won't be able for lecturing until next term. When the time comes, prepare what you're prepared to say, read it, and then say, 'Class over' and walk out. Don't wait for any questions.'

Of course, I had known that Paddy had been very ill long before Jimmy brought him to our home. He had been in hospital for quite some time. Jimmy had visited him then, and he had heard that the diagnosis was cancer. One lung, or part of it, had to be removed, and it was touch-and-go as to whether he would survive. It so happened that Jimmy's first cousin, Margaret Kean, a gentle and compassionate soul from west Clare, was a nurse in the hospital, and she had helped care for Paddy. She visited us now and then at Priory Grove and told us how he was doing. She would laugh with wry understanding when she retold the offhand remarks Paddy made to the nurses.

One day, they were told to prepare for a visit from an important dignitary, Dr John Charles McQuaid, the Arch-bishop of Dublin.[5] When Paddy heard about this, he asked Margaret to remind him of the Ten Commandments. She replied that she could remember only the seven gifts of the Holy Ghost.

Everything had to be scrubbed cleaner than clean. In due course, the Archbishop arrived with his entourage and paraded down to Paddy's bed. Paddy said he could only think he was about to die, and the Archbishop had come to hear his last confession. Paddy wondered to Margaret if this was done so that the Irish people could be told that the poet had died repentant and sorry for any remarks he had made against the Church. He told Margaret that he was not repentant, that someone had to speak up or the train would be off the tracks. Paddy was a countryman, and now and again his plain 'spake' made that clear.

To Paddy's relief, the Archbishop was quite pleasant and did not mention any of his failings. He prayed over him and left as quickly as he had appeared. Paddy tried to recall what had been said. Had McQuaid said something about giving him a small grant? In any event, soon afterwards Paddy had a visit from some big shots from the university. He thought they had hinted at an honorary doctorate. Paddy wondered if he had to stay alive to receive it, or could it be conferred posthumously. They told him they were not yet in a position to make any promises, but that at the very least there would be a lectureship. Paddy realized that he would need to be alive to get that. But, as he himself told me after coming to Priory Grove, having to deliver the lectures was a fate almost worse than death.

After the visits from the dignitaries, the other patients began to realize that the patient who was so ill that all the curtains were drawn around his bed was someone impor-tant. Word got around that it was Patrick Kavanagh the poet. Paddy rallied, and, as he improved, he often held forth to his fellow 'inmates'.

'It's as good as being in the pub,' one of them told Jimmy. 'Of course,' he said, 'there's no beer, but who needs beer when the repartee is this good?'

One day, as I was putting my little Jaja into her pram to go out to the shops, Paddy said, 'I'll come with ye.'

I looked at the cut of him, his long greying hair and stubble. He was wearing Pawdge, the old tweed trousers, which by then were like a soft, baggy and crumpled duster.

'Well,' I said, 'if you think you're well enough, but you'd better wear Jim's old sports coat – it may turn cold.'

We set off for Stillorgan, me pushing the pram, Paddy hanging on my elbow. We went to a crafts store there called 'Nimble Fingers', and I selected some wools to make a cardigan jacket for Jacqueline.[6] Paddy felt the texture and commented on the colour. He told me he could crochet and that he had crocheted hats, coats, skirts and blankets for his sisters' dolls. He looked for bootlaces and asked where he could buy soft calf's leather, and the assistant gave him a phone number to call. Paddy had served his time working as a cobbler in his father's shoemaking business, so I was not surprised when he suggested buying strong, thick thread to sew on buttons and buckles.

From there, we went across to a grocery shop, and Paddy helped me select scallions, carrots, potatoes, corn, mint, parsley, garlic, and cuts of lamb. But as we walked home slowly, his breathing a little laboured, he said: 'Let's rest for a while.' We had come to a meadow we called Beaufield. Paddy walked into the long grass, lay down, and turned over on his back.

'Aren't you going to take a rest?' he asked.

So I put the brake on the pram and sat down on the grass, my legs tucked under me sideways.

'No!' he said. 'You should stretch out on your back. That way you can hear the wind calling the land to life.'

So I did, wondering what the neighbours would say about a respectable woman lying on her back in a field with a man who looked like a down-and-out tramp.

'Look at the clouds,' Paddy said. 'You know you're moving too.' After a moment he sighed, 'Ah, the skies we travel under, it's a strange unique wonder.'

I looked up at the sky and relaxed. 'What does it matter,' I said, 'if the day goes by and nothing gets done?'

'What do you mean nothing gets done? Everything is getting done. Life is returning. The grass is growing, the bluebells tingling, the insects, the ants busy as they tend to the sleeping earth. Hear the poplars whistle ...' His voice trailed off.

I wondered if he'd fallen asleep, and indeed he had. The baby, too, was sleeping, and I was in danger of drifting off myself while I was savouring the sweetness of the meadow, the birds busy building their nests, the bluebottles buzzing, the butterflies alighting ever so softly. Could Paddy hear them? Maybe they were the answer to the silent listener. Drops of rain on my face woke me up.

'Paddy,' I said.

'Shush, don't disturb the happenings of the land. It's so good to be part of all this. It's such a joy.'

'Yes,' I said, 'but the ground is cold, and we're going to be drenched if we don't get moving.'

We hurried, slowly, back to the house. Paddy's breathing was worrying me. I got him to bed with two hot-water bottles as soon as we got home.

Every now and then, Jimmy picked up Paddy's mail from his flat. One evening he had to call Larry to help him unload the car. Several canvas sacks tied up with wire and addressed with luggage labels were thrown in through the hall door.

'What's this, what's this?' Paddy asked as Larry dragged the sacks across the floor to him.

'They have your name on the labels, and they're tied up too tight to open,' Larry said.

'What could it be? We'll find out with the "scur" of a knife,' said Paddy. 'Margot, get me a knife from the kitchen, or a scissors.'

Paddy slashed the top of one of the bags and pulled out a handful of letters. His weary hand reached in again and out came another handful. There was a posted notice on the side of each bag with '*The Observer*' printed on it.

'Oh,' said Paddy, 'do you know what? They did ask me last October to adjudicate a poetry competition. They sent me a small cheque in advance, half the fee. I'm supposed to get the rest when I pick the winner. I'll have to send it back, but I have it already spent! I'm not up to this. I thought there'd be a couple of hundred entries, but there must be over a thousand here. I can't do it. Even opening the envelopes would wear me out. We must send them back.'

'Yes,' I said, 'you can just say you were ill.'

'I could open them and read them to you,' Margot offered.

'Yes,' Larry said, 'we'll read them aloud to you, Paddy, and then you'll only have to decide.'

'It's not that easy,' Paddy said. 'It's not easy at all to pick a poem. Oh, shit, there probably isn't a real one in the whole damn lot! But I could use the money.'

Larry broke open a letter and read a verse.

'It's no good,' Paddy said. 'It's not a poem.'

'Listen to this one.' Margot read another.

'It's no use,' said Paddy, collapsing back in the chair.

'This one is typed,' Larry said. Margot read it out loud.

'It's just shit,' Paddy pronounced.

I was clearing the table for supper and trying to keep the shitty poems out of my way. Paddy was drooping sideways, weary and downhearted, but smiling at the children. Jimmy, who had just brought in the last of the sacks, went to his desk, took a sheet of paper and wrote: 'Patrick Kavanagh is convalescing after a bout of pneumonia at 47 Priory Grove, Stillorgan, County Dublin. He will attend to the poetry competition in God's own time.'

Paddy signed the letter. It was enveloped and addressed, and Larry was dispatched to the post box down the road.

Paddy bucked up and pulled in his chair. The evening lamb stew, full of scallions and potatoes, carrots and peas, was dished up and demolished with satisfaction. From that evening on, whenever there was a lull in activities, the poems would be read and sorted. There were two piles; one designated 'Work in Progress', the other 'Shit'. Most were in the pile marked 'Shit'. Finally, one night, Paddy jumped up and cried out, 'We have it! We have a poem, a real poem. Margot, read it for your father. Betty, come and listen. We've found a poem. Imagine, in all that pile we found a poem. All the rest can be thrown away.'

Jimmy said he thought the poems should be sent back to the editor, and that he would deal with it in the morning.

He started putting them back into their envelopes and bundling them up in elastic bands. Then the winning poem was clapped in a large, important envelope, and addressed to the administrator of the competition, and Paddy wrote a statement which was enclosed with the poem. Again, Larry was dispatched to the post box down the road. Paddy gave a sigh of relief.

To tell the truth, I was a little taken aback. Later that night I asked Jimmy if Paddy had really found a poem.

'Well, he found his poem, and that was what they asked him to do. But don't let it worry you. He did a mountain of work for a very small fee. Anyway, I'm sending the whole lot back, and they can search for another poem if they don't like the one he picked.'

'Fair enough,' I said sleepily.

Paddy was back in action. With Margot acting as secretary, he wrote the odd review, and now and then a few lines of poetry. And then there was the conundrum of what he called 'Tierney's fucking cheques', the payment for lectures Paddy delivered in UCD. It came from the then president of the college, Professor Michael Tierney, and it had to be collected each month.

We were now in early April, and Paddy was getting stronger. He had taken to sitting on an old school stool that was halfway down the garden among the Brussels sprouts and parsley. Every now and then he'd come to the kitchen window and ask, 'Are the children back yet? When they come back, send them down to me. I'm lonely, so very lonely.'

In his demeanour and longing, I clearly saw the man who had written:

> Great God above
> Must I forever be a dream of love?
> Must I forever see as in a glass
> The loveliness of life before me pass
> Like Anna Quinn or sunlight on the grass? [7]

'But Paddy,' I said, 'spring is here, and things are getting better.'

'I know, I know. Send the children down,' he said before ambling back to the cabbages and buttercups.

We had a dog called Tigo, and in the afternoon when he heard the school bell ringing, he would start jumping and scratching at the door. I'd wait a few minutes and let him out. He'd tear up the road looking for the children. Margot and EllyMay, with Margot hauling her sister's books as well as her own, would be first to arrive home, then Larry would arrive on his bicycle, with Tigo racing beside him. EllyMay, who never went in a door if she could climb through a window or over the garage, would call out in her high, sweet voice, 'Paddy, I'm home. See I'm cartwheeling across the grass. Look at me.'

Paddy would often propose an after-school walk, and EllyMay was very happy to agree.

'Margot,' she would say, 'me and Paddy are going to the beautiful Beaufielder's field. Do you want to come?'

'It's not "me and Paddy are going", it's "Paddy and I are going," ' Margot corrected her.

'And me too,' came EllyMay's reply.

Margot's teacher had told the class to bring in a sign of spring. Margot selected chestnut tree candles as her sign of spring. EllyMay was then, as she still is, an ardent lover and student of wildflowers. The two girls and Paddy would make off over the dyke at the end of our garden, and I would ask Larry to go with them so Paddy would have help walking if he got tired. Off they all went with the dog, through the briars and the brambles, pushing aside the thistles and nettles to get out onto the Beaufield meadows. Such excitement, as if they were the very first to discover cowslips and buttercups, prim-roses, poppies not yet popped, and the clovers and the long barley grasses and the weed called lady's lace and Paddy's 'violent wild iris'. They'd get back with armfuls of wild every-thing. Only the stickybacks were truly unwelcome (because they attached themselves as an outer layer to Jimmy's old tweed trousers, and got brought back to the house where they got deposited all over the chairs).[8] Each day's collec-tion of long grasses, rushes, Michaelmas daisies, dandelions and forget-me-nots were arranged in jam-jars on my mantel-pieces to 'please mammy'. Of all the children, Paddy was the most wildly happy. Where had the loneliness gone?

As the days went by, the children were becoming more and more involved with whatever Paddy was doing, and the whys and wherefores of all these happenings. He built a separate relationship with each of them. I could see how interested they were, and I could feel the influence he was having. EllyMay had gone wild about flowers and God. One day she came to me with a huge bunch of hydrangeas.

'Where did you get those?' I asked in some alarm.

'I found them growing wild on somebody's bush' was the child's reply. But I knew they must have come from our neighbour's garden.

'Now, Betty,' Paddy cut in, 'flowers have a right to grow wherever they like. They grow to give delight, especially to children. People shouldn't try to contain them in square gardens. EllyMay is helping them escape.'

'Well,' I said to EllyMay, 'I'm escaping out to see Mrs Moroney. I think I'll take these fresh scones as a peace offering. You and Paddy can do without them at teatime.'

EllyMay had taken to seeking out Paddy any chance she got. 'Me and Paddy' became her refrain: 'Me and Paddy want to know when supper will be ready'; 'Me and Paddy want some wire to tie up the sweet peas'; 'Me and Paddy think we need to fix the heels of Larry's boots'. And I also got: 'Paddy is teaching me a poem. Want to hear it?' To this day, EllyMay loves to recite 'The One', a poem that Paddy himself taught her.

Green, blue, yellow and red –
God is down in the swamps and marshes,
Sensational as April and almost incred-
    ible the flowering of our catharsis.
A humble scene in a backward place
Where no one important ever looked;
The raving flowers looked up in the face
Of the One and the Endless, the Mind that has baulked
The profoundest of mortals. A primrose, a violet,
A violent wild iris – but mostly anonymous performers,
Yet an important occasion as the Muse at her toilet

Prepared to inform the local farmers
That beautiful, beautiful, beautiful God
Was breathing His love by a cut-away bog.[9]

One day EllyMay came running in to say, 'Me and Paddy are putting up a trellis, and we're going to grow a whole bunch of sweet peas along the trellis, so you'll have beautiful flowers.'

I wondered at Paddy's patience. Like most young children, EllyMay had a hundred and one questions. Paddy always answered her, and she loved to learn poems from him. She took great pride in learning the meaning of words that were new to her. And there were many of the words in 'The One' that were new to her then.

'Sen-sa-tional,' she said. 'I don't know what that means.'

'Of course you do,' Paddy said. 'You smell, you see, you hear, you taste, you feel. Your senses respond to the creation. All the aromas of your mammy's cooking, all the scents of the flowers, the lilacs, the lavenders, the roses, all the music from the birds, all the warmth of the sun, all the colours from the rainbow. Ah, there's a lovely breeze now. Do you feel it blowing through your hair?'

'Yes. And I feel it when I dance. I wear my hair in a ponytail and daddy always calls it a cock's tail. When I dance, I can feel it flying behind me. Is that sensational, Paddy?'

'Surely,' was Paddy's amused answer. 'And here is another new word for you – *catharsis*. When things change, when a poppy pops, when a flower unfolds, when talk turns to laughter, when laughter fills a room with joy, when joy bursts forth in song, when a hairy molly turns into a moth, when a moth spins silk for its cocoon, when a weaver weaves, when a seamstress sews a long silk robe. Everything keeps changing. There is a presence. Rest on it. Lean on it. It will support you.'

Paddy's relationship with Larry was 'man to man'. I saw them surveying the garden together like a pair of old gardeners, and I overheard them talking about their plans. Paddy thought they should turn over a few sods to make a bed for vegetables. Was there a spade? Larry said it was in the coalhouse. What about a hoe? They discussed the need for that. Paddy said potatoes were his favourite vegetable. You couldn't have your dinner without them. They discussed that too. Paddy said the drills should be dug at the bottom of the garden where the drainage was good. The drills had to be straight, so they agreed to mark out the lines with a cord. Paddy said that Larry would start digging with the spade because he had the strength for the job, and Paddy would break up the clods with the hoe. Larry said his father had just bought boxes of seeds and seedlings for carrots, cabbage and onions, so while they were at it, they should plant them too, along with the potatoes. Paddy said, 'Your mother uses lots of herbs, so we'll keep this patch here for parsley, mint, basil and maybe lemon-breath.' That was the name he had for what is commonly called lemon balm.

Paddy often read to Margot what he had written. She liked the beautiful words strung together. I remember him saying 'Now I want a word that goes with bird.'

And she said, 'Well, it's there in what you said Paddy: word and bird.'

'Well then, how about something that goes with hedges and ditches?'

She said, 'How about landscapes in stitches? You know I like a tapestry. Are you writing a poem, Paddy?'

'No, it's more like being a wordsmith. The word must fit, but it must have sound, mood, feeling and meaning. Poetry is not easy. It's best when it just happens.'

'Oh, you mean like it happens when you paint a water-colour?'

Paddy said, 'Well, I haven't tried watercolours, but it's the same for an artist: it's best when it just happens.'

Paddy liked to lift Jaja out of her pram and take her for a walk around the garden. She would hold onto his finger, her other hand clutching Tigo's hair as he too slowed his steps to suit hers. The first word she mastered was Margot. She was so pleased when her daddy clapped his hands with delight that, from then on, she added an 'o' to the end of names. So it was Mammo, Daddo, Larro; and our little Norfolk terrier, origi-nally called Tiger because of his red brown colour, became Tigo. Paddy was well on his way to 'Paddo'.

It was about this time that Larry arrived home one day, tired and distraught. His bicycle had been stolen, and he had had to walk home all the way from the Merrion Church. He had just left it for a minute while he went in to say a prayer and when he came out it was gone. I was really upset.

'How could you let that happen?' I said, adding with a total lack of logic, 'Even if you did go in to say a prayer, you should have taken the bike in with you. Now what are you going to do? You'll have to walk to school every day. It's all of four miles.' Larry started to cry and defend himself. So I took a different tack. 'Well,' I said, 'we'll say a prayer to Saint Anthony, and you can light candles.' I trailed off helplessly.

Paddy was in the living room. He stepped right out in the hubbub.

'There's no use crying and praying. Just curse them into hell and out of it. Get it out of your system and then settle down to figure out if there is anything you can do,' said Paddy, as he offered his version of consolation to the distraught child.

'Yes,' I said, 'you can say a prayer to Saint Anthony and make a report to the police and –'

'Say a prayer to the police? Light a fire under them! Forget it. They won't do a frigging thing. Now if your Ferrari was stolen, that'd be another matter.'

'Paddy,' I said, 'don't talk like that in front of the boy.'

'Well, he should know the truth, not to be throwing good effort after bad. I think you should kiss the bike goodbye.'

'No!' howled Larry, 'me and daddy put that bike together. That's the only bike I want.'

'Well,' Paddy said. 'I can understand that. It was a curious bike. A mongrel bike with those two huge red rubber handlebars.'

Larry sobbed, broken-hearted. 'That's my bike! It went so fast. It's the only bike I want.'

'Shush, shush!' I said, 'maybe you and your dad will put another bike together and maybe you'll make it go faster.'

Paddy said, 'Forget it, don't upset yourself. Whoever took it was a blackguard.'

We lit candles and Larry told his school friends and got great sympathy because they all knew the bike and agreed that it was the fastest bike around. They promised to be on the lookout for it. Then one Saturday, as the Angelus was ringing in the middle of the day, the phone rang. I didn't know who the caller was, but he knew me.

'Mrs O'Toole,' he said, 'Larry's bike is down here in Mount Merrion and the fellas that have it are playing handball against the back wall.'

'Are you sure it's Larry's bike?'

'Yes. I'd know it anywhere with the red rubber handle-bars,' and then the phone went dead.

I told Paddy and asked him should I call the police.

'Not at all,' he answered, and he went to the back garden where Jimmy was gardening. 'Jim, I know where Larry's bike is. Let's go.'

And away they went, found the thieves playing handball against a wall near the church, stopped only to pick up the bike and hoist it onto the back of the car, and came home in high glee, telling and retelling how they had stolen their own bike.

'They ran after us all the way up the road shouting: 'Robbers, bring back our bike! We'll call the police.'

'That's a great bike. It was a great heist. I feel so good,' said Paddy. He laid his hand on the handlebars, threw his leg over the saddle, and off he went wobbling down the road humming to himself, with Larry running beside him.

Patrick Kavanagh was consumed with a sense of the presence of God. It was not just that he believed in God, as I did. It was that he was aware of God's presence in all things. This did not make him a 'Holy Mary', or give him a 'holier than thou' attitude. On the contrary, as far as I could see he allowed himself to be as free as the breeze to say whatever he liked and do as he wished. His language was not what you expected, or indeed wanted, to hear. But you were aware at times of a painful detachment in him, a draining effort of contemplation of things too 'bizarre and beautiful' – a questioning: 'Why are we so favoured to be gazing at such marvels? How could this God be? What manner of God came with all this creative flow: the flowers, the butterflies, the creepy-crawlies, the hovering dragonflies, the gliding seagulls, the enchantment of it all?' Paddy loved Gerald Griffin's 'To a Sea-Gull' and enjoyed listening to my children recite it from memory.[10]

> White bird of the tempest! O beautiful thing,
> With the bosom of snow, and the motionless wing,
> Now sweeping the billow, now floating on high …

Like much of Paddy's own poetry, this poem explicitly evokes a supernatural connection with nature, and examples are obvious in lines such as: 'Like the spirit of Charity brooding o'er pain … Like an angel descending to comfort the world! … Like a pure spirit, true to its virtue and faith'.

Paddy's mindfulness of the presence of God, so evident in his poetry, also showed up in his conversations with my children. I was seldom part of those conversations, but I listened through my open kitchen window whenever I could.

'What I'd like to know is what makes the plants grow,' Larry asked Paddy one day as they were planting herbs by the side of the coalhouse.

'That's where God comes in,' Paddy said.

'How do you know that?'

'That's a mystery.'

'But how did you find it out?'

'Well,' Paddy said, 'thinking back on it, I wasn't thinking at all. Everything just grew and I paid no heed to the why of it. Then, one day when I was about nine, I was running through the fields, and I stumbled. I could say I stumbled on God. Because when I got up, He was there. I mean I was aware He was there. He was everywhere, all over the fields, the banks and the uplands, the hedges and ditches. I looked at the buttercups and the Michaelmas daisies, and I ran all the way down to the cut-away bog where nobody ever went.' And of course, Larry knew well, as did EllyMay, Paddy's description of God breathing love on nature in his poem 'The One'.

Another day, as I shook out the mats and brushed them down, I could hear EllyMay having one of her deep confiding chats with Paddy.

'So He is sitting with us? And is there enough room for Him? Is He up on the trees and in the clouds?'

'Yes, He loves the trees and the clouds,' Paddy said.

'Is He in the coal house?'

'He is.'

'And what is He doing in there?'

'I really don't know.'

'I'll go and see.'

And off she went and spent a few minutes in the coal house before returning to Paddy.

'Tigo is asleep in there. God must be minding him.'

'I'd say you're right.'

Eavesdropping on these conversations between Paddy and EllyMay, I often thought about remarks I had heard as a child from older people about how someone who seemed a little 'different' could 'hit the nail on the head' and give a simple explanation for some mysterious problem.

'He must have a sixth sense,' they would say.

Did Patrick Kavanagh have a sixth sense that gifted him to feel God's presence? And did this gift involve efforts of intense reflection as he gathered to himself the visions of the simple beauty in ordinary things? Or had the earth put a spell over him to compose his poetry so all of us could feel, with him, the loveliness of the world – a bank of primroses in wildest profusion. Why were we so favoured to be gazing at such marvels, and did God inspire him to write poetry to help us see the beauty and wonder of the world – the miracle of life in everyday things? What a creative genius God must be to keep it all going on, and on, and on, and on ...

My Jimmy was a morning person. Anytime round five or six he'd jump out of bed, turn on the music and dance all over the house. A handsome, athletic man of six foot three, he was light on his feet, and I thought him a better dancer than Gene Kelly. He had grown up with sisters who used to rush at him with pillows trying to deflate his enthusiasm. My own sisters threw shoes at him when he danced through their bedroom one summer morning in Kilkee. He used to swim across the bay before breakfast. In Dublin, he'd swim from the Forty Foot to Dun Laoghaire pier and back again.[11] He not only had a joyous, energetic spirit; he had an impulsive one. If anyone suggested 'wait a moment, let's think about this,' they were brushed aside like a fly with a wave of the hand. Procrastination was never an option with him.

As I was growing up, my father used to say, 'You must take the ball on the hop.' Taking the ball on the hop with Jim O'Toole while I was young and single had led to a very active, 'good times' kind of life, but with four children and a recovering Paddy to look after, I was put to the pin of my collar trying to keep my life on an even keel. 'Easy does it' was becoming my motto. You can imagine how my new philosophy of life was blown away when Jimmy jumped out of bed one bright April morning, calling out: 'It's a beautiful morning. Paddy, you're better! Girls, pull something on, we're off to the races. Larry, forget about school. Wear your boots, the going is soft, and the fields may be muddy. It's going to be a wonderful day. Betty, put a few cakes of bread in a basket – and a jar of pickles. Don't go to any trouble. The milkman has just come. I'll put a crate in the car. Paddy, Punchestown races are today.[12] It's going to be great. Throw something on. We'll meet everyone. The Hartys have a horse running. Martin Molony is up. Vincent O'Brien …'

'Can I bring the dog?' Larry called.

'Why not?'

'How about some friends?'

'No,' I cut in, 'just eat a good breakfast, everyone. Margot, when you are ready, dress Jaja. Everyone should bring a jacket. Paddy, dress warmly. EllyMay, we must get ready quickly, so they don't go without us.'

'Can we wear the Easter bonnets Aunt Kitty sent us?' Margot called.

'Wear anything you can find,' Jimmy called back. 'I'm going to put petrol in the car and buy the papers. Be ready when I get back. We mustn't miss the first race.'

When he returned, we all jumped in the car, and this was how I found ourselves barrelling down the road. Jimmy and Paddy were in the front, chuckling and gossiping. I was in the back with the four children and the dog. I was listening to Larry telling the girls about the goings-on at his school, and I was also trying to pick up odd snatches of gossip from the front. We were coming to the bend where the Mabel Young beech trees framed the road. Paddy was saying 'I saw her last exhibition. They say she is in love and getting married to Paul Henry.'[13]

'I have her "Carn Lake". Remind me to show it to you,' Jim answered.

The car whipped round the bend. I smiled out the window. I was so pleased. It seemed we were leaving winter's woes behind and racing towards light summer lands. How bright everywhere looked, how good life was!

The Punchestown Festival is the major horse racing festival of the racing season, and it has the flavour and excitement of all the counties of Ireland. It is the first big race meeting of spring and attracts a huge influx of horsey people from all around the country. It has more of everything: more people, more talk, more tips, more entries, higher jumps, greener grass, more style, more stables, more stalls covered with all kinds of fruits and candies and tended by the colourful women of Moore Street, more bookies and tick-tack men.

We parked the car on the top of the hill and raced down towards the excitement, Jacqueline on Jimmy's shoulders holding tight to his hair; Paddy running with his hand on Larry's shoulder, Larry's arm around his waist; Margot and EllyMay, looking lovely in their new Easter bonnets, running hand-in-hand headlong after the dog. I was only running to catch up and saying, 'Please go easy. There's plenty of time.'

'There's plenty of time,' said a man passing, 'but if you don't hurry up, you'll be late.'

Paddy was much stronger now and highly pleased with himself and all round him. As we slowed down a little, I saw Jimmy slip a few notes to Paddy. I looked away – after all it was only money.

We were having breathless conversations with friends from all over.

'Isn't it great to be out for the day?' I called out to Maura McGuinan, an old friend of mine.

'And leave the house behind,' she called back.

'And your worries,' someone added.

'It's great altogether to feel the grass under your feet.'

Someone was singing a song I knew well:

> Dear thoughts are in my mind
> And my soul it soars enchanted,
> As I hear the sweet lark sing
> In the clear air of the day. [14]

We set up our blankets and picnic on a grassy spot with a good view of the racetrack, ran back and forth to the parade ring between races, and immersed ourselves in the whole scene – the jockeys in their colours tap-slapping their spats and booted legs, the bookies sign-talking to their tick-tack men, Maggie Men vying for attention with noisy stable boys and horse trainers.[15] At lunchtime, hunger proved a great sauce for our 'no trouble picnic', and then it was back to the races and meeting friends.

All too soon the races were winding down. Margot and Larry had gone off with their dad. I had inherited EllyMay, much to her chagrin. She would have much preferred to be with Paddy. She and I were like two goats tied together, pulling in different directions. We were making our way over the now rutted and flattened grass, strewn with sweet wrappers and discarded race-cards when, all of a sudden, EllyMay put her eye on a Maggie Man's stall.

'Mammy, Mammy, look at all the pretty-deasies!'[16]

'We have to go. Look around for daddy,' I said firmly.

We did look around, and there was Paddy coming up the hill holding a closed fist high.

'I won. I won. Can you believe I won?' he was shouting, and his winnings were protruding out of his fist.

EllyMay broke from me and rushed into his arms.

'Paddy, Paddy, come and see,' she said as she dragged him to the stall. 'See all the pretty-deasies, rings and things, and dollies, whirligigs. See! See!'

Paddy was as much a child as EllyMay.

'Yes,' he said, 'I do see all the pretty-deasies. Isn't this the wonder of all time? A ring-go-thing, a ting-a-ling, a gladdy bell,[17] a ding-dong bell, a tick-tock clock, a wand – could it be a magic wand? – tin whistles, mouth organs, a tumbling monkey, a merry-go-round, jacks-in-boxes, Russian dollies, a horn, a wind-up dancing Mopsy,[18] flying birdies on a stick.'

'Ha, ha! A flying canary!' he cried with glee as he whirled the stick.

'Make up yer minds,' said the Maggie Man. 'I'm in a hell of a hurry. I have to pack up.'

'We're buying! Can't you see we're buying,' said Paddy, waving his fist of notes.

'Look Paddy, a *cead agam* dolly. He's asking permission to go to the toilet,' said the delighted EllyMay.[19]

'Hello! Dolly! We must have dollies,' Paddy declared with amusement.

'What price the googaws?[20] Let's have a look at what's in the box. I'll give a shilling for this,' said Paddy, holding up a clock.

'Go on outta that!' the Maggie Man said. 'That clock is half a crown, five bob for the bigger one.[21] I have to be going. I'll not have any dilly-dallying. Away with ye.'

'We're buying,' said Paddy.

'You are in your hat. Oh, sweet saints, make up yer minds. I have to be off.'

EllyMay wound up the Mopsy and set it off dancing.

'Let's make a deal. I'll buy the whole bleddy lot from you for what's here in my fist,' said Paddy with his hand held high above his head. 'Stall and all,' he added.

The man's eyes fastened on Paddy's fist, trying to see what types of notes were in it.

'I don't know what's in your fist. These are valuable.'

'And I don't know the value of your valuables,' said Paddy, 'isn't that the fun of it? Do we ever know what's in store for us? Isn't life full of surprises?' His fist stayed high and tight. 'Fair exchange is no robbery. Do we have a deal?'

'We do! We do!' said the Maggie Man, reaching up and pulling Paddy's fist down to his knees and prying it open. There were at least two ten-pound notes, a twenty, a fiver and more.

'Have we gone clean out of our minds?' I gasped.

'That we have, Ma'am,' said the Maggie Man who now had all the notes in his hand. 'I'll be wishing good luck to ye.'

Paddy had bought a whole menagerie. EllyMay's eyes were overflowing with ecstasy. Paddy's magnificence had put him on top of the world, and he sang to EllyMay:

> Two for a penny
> Will anyone buy
> The finest ballads ever made
> From the stuff of joy?[22]

Jimmy turned up with Larry and Margot, and Paddy ordered the car to be brought around so 'EllyMay's valuables' could be loaded.

'Right, sir,' Jimmy replied, saluting smartly.

Margot and Larry were checking out the valuables with applauding squawks.

'Frisbees!' said Larry. 'We'll train Tigo to catch them.'

'Rolly Bowlies,' said Margot, 'and look at all the dollies.'[23]

Everyone was in a hilariously joyous mood. I decided to join the nonsense, the madness, a surprisingly wondrous happening, and pretend that the theatrics were not too much for me. The celebrations were at such a high pitch, people were stopping to congratulate us.

'Did ye win all this?' some asked, understandably, for what other explanation could there be for the mounds of 'valuables' that were stuffed into, and on top of, the car? As Jimmy and a passer-by were tying the stall onto the roof of the car, I got in the car to feed my Jacqueline. The dog jumped in after me. Margot and Larry started stuffing the 'valuables' round me. Every time I moved, the little rubber *Cead Agam* dolly squeaked. The feathers from the 'canary-on-a stick' were bothering the dog and making her bark. The Rolly Bowlies were strung around Paddy's neck. EllyMay had a ring on every finger, and 'all the wonders of the world' were jingling around the top of the car as we bumped across the fields.

I tried to listen to Paddy and Jimmy's long, highbrow discourse on the magical value of money when it can buy joy and delight. Jimmy burst into his favourite song and we all joined in:

> Happy days are here again,
> The skies above are clear again,
> So let's sing a song of cheer again,
> Happy days are here again.
> Altogether, shout it now.
> There's no one
> Who can doubt it now,
> So let's tell the world about it now –
> Happy days are here again.[24]

When we got home, I set about putting a 'no trouble' supper on the table. Everyone else got busy organizing all the 'valuables' in the hall to make a Tin Pan Alley and Fun

Palace, with a hurdy-gurdy musical section. Friends and relatives and, of course, neighbours would eventually have to be invited in to see it. At five a.m. the next morning, the tick-tock clock started to alarm at an alarming volume. My goodness, I thought, the baby will wake. I stumbled down the stairs into the Tin Pan Alley to look for the offending tick-tocker. Margot came down after me and sat on the stairs.

'I'm sorry about the hall, Mammy.'

'You're sorry, love? It's not your fault at all. It's those two crazy men, your dad and Paddy Kavanagh. You know they're crazy, don't you?'

'Yes, Mammy, but it is a nice kind of craziness.' She hugged her knees and the happiest of smiles spread across her face.

Maybe, I thought, joy is worth buying after all. I put my arms around my little girl. 'Let's forget about the hall and enjoy Tin Pan Alley but first let's get back to bed and sleep for another hour or so.'

One evening Jimmy was writing a five-minute talk for the radio, Jaja was beside him in her go-car, and Paddy was at the other end of the table tapping on his typewriter. EllyMay was trying to set the same table for supper, and Margot was doing her homework but at the same time giving instructions.

'Put the fork on the left, leave a space for the plate, then the knife on the right.'

EllyMay was blessing herself at each place setting. This was her method of distinguishing her right from her left. When she got to her father, she said: 'I think you'll have to move over. I need to set a place for God.'

'Oh,' said Jimmy, 'I think God can fit over there between yourself and Larry.'

'No, no! He's very important. He must be very big. Do you know how big He is?'

'I suppose I could say "He is all over", but I'm busy now and I think we could leave that question for the boys in Rome.'

'Who are those boys?' asked Larry.

'The red hats,' says Paddy.

'They're talking about the cardinals,' said Margot.

Paddy offered, 'They're too busy chasing scientists like your dad. They have little time for EllyMay's important concerns.'

'Well,' I said, 'when I was in college, my professor of philosophy was Father McGrath of the White Friars, and he was also a professor at Maynooth College. He used to say that the Church rights itself every so often. They just have to be sure that the scientists are right before they agree with them.'[25]

'Once every century,' Jimmy commented.

'Our science teacher says that if we leave it to the Church, they will have the world flattened in no time,' Larry added.

'Please,' I said, 'I am a teacher, and I don't want to hear how you pupils quote us.'

I tried to steer the conversation away from the cardinals, the scientists and God himself. Patrick Kavanagh was now part of the family, and since he joined, we had been having God for breakfast, dinner and supper. Over the years any of us who had followed Kavanagh's writings or listened to his poetry could not be surprised to find that the man was preoccupied with God. He was prepared to quote Teresa of Ávila, Saint John of the Cross, and indeed many others. Jimmy was more widely read and, having been trained by the Jesuits, he was schooled in debate – he had been to some of Teilhard de Chardin's lectures to engineers at Aurora University.[26] Being a scientist, he had closely followed the controversy on evolution, which was raging at that time, just as it is today. Both men delighted in language. Jimmy's humorous remarks and witty turns of phrase brought chuckles from Paddy. Paddy's keen mind and depth of interest in a wide range of subjects, especially nature, intrigued Jimmy. Paddy seemed to regard the fields and swamps, and indeed the whole world, as one huge project where God was breathing life and love all around. One of his irritations with the Church was that it seemed to be trying to take God out of the countryside and confine him to buildings – namely churches. Another was that the Catholic clergy were not allowing Irish culture and traditions enough freedom to grow. Paddy said they were imposing rules and restrictions that had no moral basis.

To illustrate his points, Paddy told us stories of actions he had seen priests take. I also told a few stories myself, such as the one about the canon who returned from vacation and was shocked to find the parishioners dancing an old-time waltz in 'his' parish hall – a hall that had been built and paid for by them. The outraged canon jumped on the stage, laid hold of the microphone and ordered, 'Let's have The Walls of Limerick: men to the right and women to the left. We will have no more of this belly-pushing. Clean dancing only,' he told the bewildered parishioners.

I also provided another example of the narrow-minded control the clergy often sought to impose on the Irish people.

This was a story from my dad, Laurence Ryan, and he told it often and with great amusement. It seems that my mother, when she was a newlywed, had invited her younger sister and a few friends from County Cork up to her new home in Cratloe, County Clare, for a weekend. Sunday turning fine and breezy, my dad suggested that they go for a picnic by the seaside at Lahinch. Of course, they took their swimming costumes, as they were called back then. My mother loved the water but was nervous of venturing out into the high waves without my dad, who was a strong swimmer. While they were out bobbing up and down on the surf, a priest appeared at the edge of the water frantically waving them to come out of the water. As they were responding to the priest's gesturing, my mother asked my dad to hurry ahead and find out why the good priest was so agitated. As my dad got within earshot, he heard the priest shouting, 'This is disgraceful. Men and women together in the water! Don't you know you're not allowed to go swimming with women?'

When my father told this story, it was easy to imagine how he, a newly married man, had enjoyed the mischievousness in the reply he quickly shot back to the priest, 'Well, I'll tell you something, Father. I slept with one of those women last night.'

'I knew you were a bad egg,' replied the sputtering priest.

This was a mainstay story in my family, told often by my father to my children as an example of just how ridiculous the clergy's attempts at control could become.

Jimmy remarked that my father's story reminded him of the Sean O'Faolain short story 'The Man Who Invented Sin'.

'Yes, indeed,' said Paddy, 'we have enough real sins. We don't need the Church inventing more for us. We should go back to what Christ said: 'This is my body, this is my blood.' He didn't say, I've taken God out of the countryside and put him in a cup.'

'Now, Paddy,' I said, 'the priests do not say that.'

'You're right,' Paddy agreed, 'they don't say it, but they act as if they'd kidnapped God, were holding him in a church, and they were the only ones who can understand or talk to him.' Then he added: 'Not all of them, of course. Just some get carried away and misunderstandings arise. I am sorry. I shouldn't talk like that in front of the children.'

'It's all right,' Margot said. 'Our teacher said that priests can make mistakes and we should speak up.'

'Our priest told us that Christ turned water into wine,' said EllyMay, 'and I told him that I can easily believe that because my daddy can turn milk into Yorkshire relish. He puts milk into the Yorkshire relish bottle, shakes it up, and out comes Yorkshire relish!'

'I think we should send that miracle on to Rome,' quipped Paddy.

'Jokes aside,' said Jimmy, 'Christ was the sum of all goodness.'

'Christ was the sum of wisdom for all men for whom he died, which was the race of man,' Paddy said.

'Are all the children in bed?/ It's now eight o'clock,' sang Jimmy, belting out the Wee Willie Winkie nursery rhyme as he lifted Jaja into his arms. 'A wee stumpie stousie who cannot say her prayers', he finished in good Scottish English, and off he went racing the kids up the stairs.[27]

45

About once a week, two Christian Brothers came to Priory Grove to reminisce about the past.[28] They sat by the fire while I made apple pie from apples they had gleefully shaken from the trees at the back of their monastery. They were both retired teachers, so they had reverted to being liberal: they felt now that the Church and the government had wrapped education up too tightly, not allowing the children to develop their minds and their culture. Paddy sometimes joined in conversation with them and enjoyed being taken back to his schooldays. I found these exchanges very interesting, and so I was somewhat annoyed when, one day, while the Brothers were reading aloud from my old National School reader, we were interrupted by the doorbell. Hoping to be able to quickly rejoin the conversation, I made my way through the Tin Pan Alley in the hall and opened the door to a lady I recognized but had never met: it was Ria Mooney, the Artistic Director of the Abbey Theatre.

'You must be Betty,' she said. 'I know Jim and his play, *Man Alive!*, of course. I've heard a rumour that I can find Patrick Kavanagh here, and I'm hoping it's true.'

As I welcomed her into the house, I felt myself flushing with the embarrassment of having this most distinguished guest see my home in such a state of undecorous decor. I explained that EllyMay and Paddy had painted what I called 'a fabulous "Jack Yeats" on my walls. Any day now they will be discovered.' But I added, 'We have a nice fire and some lively conversation going on inside, and we have two retired Christian Brothers here reading my school reader.'

When Paddy saw her, he exclaimed 'Ria!' in surprise.

Ria said, 'So here you are, Mr Patrick Kavanagh. No one has seen you around town in such a long time, and we've been searching all over for you. Finally, someone told me that you were spotted at the Punchestown races with Jimmy O'Toole.'

'I haven't been well,' Paddy said, 'but Betty has been looking after me.'

I said, 'Ria, you'll stay for tea. I've just made tarts with the apples these two Brothers brought me. They stole them from the back of their monastery.'

'I don't think I can resist an invitation like that – a good fire, an apple tart, and the best of company – but first I have to complete my mission. I need a "yes" from Patrick before any tea and tart. The Abbey is having a big reception for a large group of distinguished dignitaries from literary and theatre circles, and it just would not be fitting to have it without you, Patrick. I have been given the mission of finding you and getting you to agree to be part of the event. Will you agree to come?'

'Oh, I don't think I'd be up to it. I've not been well. All those people, a fancy formal setting – it's not my type of occasion at all. I couldn't even consider it.'

My Jimmy cut in, 'Patrick Kavanagh will be honoured to accept this wonderful invitation. Betty and I will be happy to help him prepare for this important occasion.'

'Yes,' I said. 'Now, Paddy, this gives you the perfect excuse to get a nice haircut and get all dressed up. As a matter of fact, I think I have exactly the right jacket for you to wear. It was given to Jimmy by Jack Doyle, and it was the one Jack wore when he was singing with Movita at the Theatre Royal.

Jimmy's hardly ever worn it because it's only suitable for a formal occasion such as this.'

'The Gorgeous Gael,' as Jack Doyle was known in the newspapers, was a great boxer and when he was married to Movita, the Mexican film star, they lived in Ireland for a while, which is how Jimmy knew them.[29] (When I was in college, I had gone with my sister Kitty, who had somehow laid her hands on two tickets, to a great show Jack and Movita put on. It was a wonderful night.)

Jimmy was gone in a flash and was back soon with the jacket on a hanger under tissue paper. Paddy examined the jacket with interest.

'Put it on, so we can get Ria's opinion on whether it is suitable for the occasion,' Jimmy coaxed. Paddy put on the jacket and seemed to have forgotten that he was not up for going to a formal reception. The sleeves would have to be shortened, and the shoulders fitted, but there was plenty of time to get the tailoring done. Ria invited Jimmy to the reception also. He and Paddy attended together and had a whale of a time. It turned out to be a big affair. Patrick Kavanagh was the guest of honour, and the evening was a tremendous success.

I was especially delighted that Ria Mooney and her associates in Dublin's literary society had made it a point to publicly recognize and honour Paddy. Jimmy and I, like others who were friendly with Paddy, were keenly aware of how devastated and enduringly distressed he was by the description of him published in 1952 by *The Leader*. This 'profile' of Paddy in the magazine praised his poetry but attacked him as a person.[30] Paddy filed, and subsequently lost, a libel suit in 1954. From what Paddy told me, what hurt him most about the profile was the implication that he had maligned country people. The source or sources for the profile were anonymous and remained so throughout the court case and thereafter. Not knowing who among those who claimed to know him and spend time with him had anonymously sought to damage him and misrepresent his attitudes was very unsettling for Paddy. I have no doubt, and my husband Jimmy had no doubt, that the ordeal – the publication of the profile and the ensuing litigation that spanned the years of his treatment for lung cancer – left him deeply wounded and prone to being cagey with many who presented themselves to him as his admirers. Paddy knew Jimmy for what he was: a joyful and exuberant person who did not seek to knock others. I think Paddy's confidence in Jimmy explains why he was never circumspect with Jimmy, and the friendship between them remained warm and comfortable throughout these difficult years.

Much as he would have liked to be in the court to support Paddy during the trial, Jimmy was unable to get time off work. The trial went on for days and was covered in the press, and the broad consensus was that things were going very badly for Kavanagh. On what turned out to be the last day of the trial, Jimmy called and asked me to go to the court to support Paddy. I arrived at the courthouse to see an obviously dejected Paddy standing by himself at the top of the steps outside the courthouse. He took one step and then sank down to sit on the top step.

This is our poet, our top Irish poet – why is he alone at a time like this? I thought as I made my way up the steps to him.

'Paddy, would you like to come with me to get something to eat?' I asked.

He answered in a muffled tone, 'No, I just want to be left alone. The judge is about to sum up. The case seems lost, and I'm exhausted.'

I went down the steps and round to the pub and looked for someone I knew. I recognized Des O'Driscoll, the scrum-half on Jimmy's rugby team, Bective Rangers.

'Des,' I said, 'Patrick Kavanagh is sitting on the court-house steps. I'm trying to get him something to eat. He is very downhearted. He thinks he's losing the case.'

'That he is,' Des said. 'Go back to him, and I'll join you as soon as I get some sandwiches. How many do you need?'

'Paddy is by himself,' I replied. Des registered surprise.

I went back and sat with Paddy. His head was down in his hands. He did not say a word. Des came with a tray of sandwiches and three coffees.

'You shouldn't have bothered. I can't eat,' Paddy said.

'Yes, you can,' Des said, holding out a sandwich. 'Never mind the case. Just live to fight another day.'

Paddy took the sandwich and the cup of coffee.

'Live to fight another day. I like that,' he said.

We were still on the steps when people began to file out after the jury had very quickly rendered its verdict in favour of *The Leader*. Despite having told us the case was lost, Paddy seemed stunned when he heard the news. The case was later appealed, but it was settled for a very small amount before the start of a new trial. But Paddy never got an apology, and that was what was needed to clear his name and his legacy.

Like Jimmy himself, the rest of his family, as well as many of his friends, had unconventional backgrounds and perspectives. I had many opportunities to observe how Paddy engaged with the succession of unusual people who visited Priory Grove while he was with us. Granny Elly and Grandad John O'Toole came for afternoon tea every Thursday. Both accepted Paddy as he typed away at the end of the table, drinking his tea and eating hot buttered scones.

Grandad, my father-in-law, had the demeanour of a Chief of Police, and had worked abroad in France and China before his retirement.[31] Elly was very good-looking and always well-dressed. She had good carriage, blonde hair going platinum, curls swept high to a crown, steady blue eyes, and her body language radiated a strong assumption of power. She had been principal of two schools in Shanghai, the Collège Municipal Français[32] and the Jewish Conservatory.

Once, when I had been married just a few weeks, Granny Elly took it upon herself to educate me on how to conduct myself in city life, ignoring the fact that I had been gallivanting around Dublin all the previous five years. I was dressed nicely and was on my best prim-and-proper behaviour as we boarded a crowded tram car going into town. Because I worked out that she must be close on seventy years of age, I was a little concerned that she would not get a seat. I need not have worried. One of her brothers, Patrick Bermingham, was a famous discus thrower, and another, Jack, was a champion high jumper. Granny was said to be mentally and physically stronger than they were.[33]

On the bus her powerful right hand descended on a young man's shoulder. 'Aren't you the fine young man to so quickly give up your seat to a woman?'

He was lifted out of the seat and propelled up the aisle as she plopped down on the seat.

Then she announced, 'And this is my daughter-in-law. She might be expecting a baby, so she's lucky the young gentlemen in this city have been properly brought up and she can have a choice of seats. Jump up now, boys, and let everybody see how well-mannered you are.'

Several men jumped up. Embarrassed, I modestly said my thank you.

'We're so fortunate to live in such a civilized city. Clean streets and no crime,' continued Granny, speaking with great authority and perfect diction.

Based on how she presented herself, people would quickly decide that she was somebody who should not be challenged, and few opposing opinions were ever aired. She believed that women did not need to start a movement. All they had to do was to assume the power they already possessed. She certainly was a great example of how to live by that philosophy.

In Shanghai, Grandad got a complete year off work every third year. They travelled the world: Hong Kong, Bombay, Zanzibar, South Africa, Marseille in France, Holland, San Francisco, the Santa Fé trail, New York, and London, are some of the places they visited. He had lived for lengthy periods in

Paris, Shanghai and Korea. Grandad indulged himself in long orations about life – after all, he had seen plenty of it. When the kids were home from school, I was pleased that they could hear many new and old stories with colourful descriptions of places, personalities and happenings. He told of the shocking state of Ireland as he was growing up in Lissycasey, County Clare. His grandfather had owned a farm and a mill at the time of the Great Famine. In those days, British agents under cavalry escort used to impound the grain brought to his mill by local farmers, which they had hidden in wooden coffins, and take it away to be exported. His grandfather had been caught returning 'skimmed' grain to the local people. As punishment, his grandfather had been evicted from his home and the flour mill confiscated.[34]

When Paddy heard Grandad talking about this, he stopped his typing at the kitchen table and asked, 'Why did you leave Ireland? What age were you?'

'I was sixteen. We were politically unacceptable to the authorities.[35] My father worried I might be arrested and sent in chains to the West Indies, or Australia, so I was rowed out from Galway Bay at night to a trawler going to France. I was on my way to Paris where I was supposed to go to college.'

'And did you go to college, Grandad?' Margot asked.

'I did, but I found it too hard. It was the language, you know, and then the lack of money. I stuck it out until I was eighteen. Then some of my friends were signing up for the French Foreign Legion. That seemed more exciting than the books. The choice was going off to Algeria with the Legion, or with the French International police, working in the Far

East. I went with the police and travelled to Shanghai on the Trans-Siberian Railway.'

I could never hear enough of these stories, and my kids, who would be just home from school in time for these afternoon teas, were eager to hear them too. Grandad liked me because I listened and asked questions. I was becoming detailed in my knowledge of that journey – the snow, the ice storms, the icicles hanging down off the carriage, and also hanging off the men's whiskers and the women's eyelashes. The train was transporting prisoners bound for Siberia because they had spoken against the Czar – this was long before the revolution in 1917, of course.

'We spent days and days travelling through this vast, vast land with nothing at all to see but snow. Because there weren't WCs, we had to empty buckets of slush out the windows of the train,' Grandad explained.

'What's WCs?' Larry asked.

'A WC is a water closet, a privy.'

'What's a privy?'

'The word comes from private. Now they call it a toilet.'

'Or a shit house,' Paddy put in.

'The WCs were only makeshift, and buckets of disinfectant were sloshed around the carriage.'

When Grandad eventually arrived in Shanghai, he discovered that the poor Chinese used the Yangtze River as a toilet. But in those days the city also had plenty of beautiful buildings, very different from those in the west, especially in the international Compound, which the French controlled. Grandad was kitted out in a uniform, given some training and then put on street patrol, trying to deal with the people in a mixture of pidgin English and French and some Chinese words.

One story that Grandad loved to tell, and one he told to Paddy, began with a group of Chinese children that kept pulling at his policeman sleeve saying, 'Come, come, *dépêchez-vous*, 'arry, 'arry,' which he took to mean 'hurry, hurry.'

The children pulled him down a street, pointed to an upstairs window, and then ran away. He climbed a long, narrow wooden stairs, went down a corridor and opened the first door he saw. Inside a young man lay on a bed very ill and weak with a high fever. He could hardly speak, but he seemed Irish, or maybe Welsh or Scottish.

Grandad said, 'I'll get you to a hospital. Don't bother dressing. Put your arms around my neck. I'll hoist you up on my back and we'll get a rickshaw.'

So they got down the stairs, but no rickshaw would come near them. The rickshaw drivers knew the man had cholera. The only thing Grandad could do was to set off looking for a hospital, with the patient on his back.

Granny Elly, of course, had heard this story many times before, and was displeased that her time with Paddy was being taken up having to listen to old stories from her husband.

'Don't be so long-winded, John. Get to the finish.'

'So, Paddy,' he continued ignoring his wife, 'I got to the hospital, but everyone moved away from us. There was sweat pouring off me, but then along comes a beautiful woman, a nurse. "My name is Agnes Hayley Bell," she said'.[36] And I said, "Mine is John O'Toole".

'Well, she led me to a bed, and helped me lift the man off my shoulders. His name was Gibson. I think he was from Kilkee, in County Clare. She was the best nurse ever. She nursed him back to life. But, of course, she put me in quarantine. I got the same bleddy fever, but she nursed me right through it. Do you recognize the name Agnes Hayley Bell? She was the mother of Lady Mary Haley Bell, the woman who wrote the book *Whistle Down the Wind*, and she was the wife of the great actor John Mills, and her granddaughter is Haley Mills, who is now the young movie star. I could tell you a great many stories about the interesting people who were in Shanghai with me, if only my better half would have the manners to behave herself.'

'I've no time for these rigamaroles. Get to the point if you have a point,' said my mother-in-law as she made the table shake with a sharp pounding of her fist.

Grandad started humming, and then to sing softly, as his foot tapped in time: 'And still I thought my heart would break for the girl I left behind me.'

He continued to hum as Granny turned to Paddy for sympathy. 'Do you know, Mr Kavanagh, I've travelled halfway across the world with this man and given birth to six of his children, and now he has the impertinence to keep talking and testing my patience and taking up my valuable time. Now, John, Mr Kavanagh has no time for your balderdash. He has important writings to get down on paper, so don't be interrupting him.'

Paddy said, 'No! Not so! Not so! I find your John's story damn interesting. Extraordinary in fact. How can we ever imagine what happened to all those Irish people when they had to leave Ireland? They're scattered all over the world. Someone should write about them.'

'Yes,' Granny said, 'I left Ireland and trailed with that fellow there to the ends of the earth. I had a degree in education, and I didn't have to go with him at all. I had a fine job, teaching English and history in the Sacred Heart Convent in Roscrea, County Tipperary. I had a boyfriend. We were walking out together. He was considered a good catch, but he was a bit slow getting to the point. His intentions were honourable, but not matrimonial.'

'He just liked to be seen with a good-looking woman,' Grandad said. 'Now she's wondering if she should have married the clown who never got around to asking her.' And he went back to foot-tapping under the table and humming 'The Girl I Left Behind Me'.

'Was that what happened, Granny?' Margot asked.

'Not at all,' Granny said. 'I'll tell you what happened. I was invited to a wedding of one of my friends in Kilkee. It was a holiday weekend, so I went. Your Grandad was at it. I had never seen him before, and he was handsome. He had all his hair back then. He asked me to dance, and I love to dance. So, we went flying around the hall. He was a fine dancer.'

Grandad said, 'I couldn't believe it. Here was I, John O'Toole, dancing with the loveliest girl in the world, with her hair the colour of honey, bright curls, her laughing blue eyes, her enjoyment of the dance, so light and lively, her feet as fleet as a fiddler's dream. Well, I was going to ask her for another dance, but what came out was: "Will you marry me?" '

Granny broke in, 'And I said yes, thinking it would teach that boyfriend a lesson if I went back to Roscrea with an engagement ring on my finger.'

'And, when she said "Yes," I really thought she meant it,' continued Grandad with great gusto. 'And there I was, home on leave, never imagining anyone so lovely would marry me. Still holding her hand, I went looking for the priest who was at the wedding breakfast, and asked him to marry us there and then, as I was going back to Shanghai the next morning. I had a ticket through the Suez Canal. It will be great, I told Elly.'

'So,' Granny said, 'Before I had any time to think, I was married and waving goodbye to everyone, and they were all clapping and crying.'

'Yes,' Grandad said, 'it was definitely love at first sight. We surely taught that clown in Roscrea a good lesson.'

'He wasn't a clown.' Granny stood up to make her point. 'He was actually a very nice young man, a great catch, and good-looking too.'

Grandad started to sing again, 'And still I thought my heart would break for the girl I left behind me.'

'Lucky girl she was. She wasn't foolish like me. Having to put up with this impertinence. Do you hear him, Mr Kavanagh, singing about some girl he left behind?'

'It doesn't matter a damn where he left her, or why,' said Paddy making a bid for peace. 'He didn't marry her anyway. And you didn't want to marry the clown in Roscrea. All you wanted was for him to ask you, so that you could have the satisfaction of turning him down.'

There was a scart of a laugh from Elly O'Toole.

'You may be right, but I'm never wrong. I want no more impudence from either of you. Jimmy, I cannot stand the insubordination around here. Drive me home immediately.'

'We'll drop by Roscrea and show that clown your rings,' said Grandad with joviality, and they left with a flourish.

After they'd gone, Paddy clapped his hands with a shout of exhilaration. 'Oh, the poetry of life! The tell-tales tandem of married life. What a pair! Whipping up the flames of passion just for the hell of it.'

'Was there a girl left behind?' asked EllyMay.

'And was it Agnes Hayley Bell?' asked Margot.

'I doubt it,' I replied. 'Grandad sings that song just to drive your Granny mad, and to keep the fires from past passions blazing. At the end of all Grandad's stories there is a girl he must leave behind, and it's her heart that is broken.'

'And what happened to the Roscrea clown?' Larry wondered.

'Oh, she was just leading him up the garden path,' I decided.

'She would have led him a fine dance,' Paddy laughed. 'She'd have made a man of him.'

Jimmy's older sister, Eileen, was another very unusual character. In her own eyes she was above the rest of us. She was a violinist and played in the RTÉ and BBC orchestras. She could not do any household chores because her nails had to be kept in top condition for performances. She had been a talented child who was spoiled, and then matured into a spoiled adult who never considered anyone but herself. With Jimmy, she took it for granted that she could ask of him whatever she wished whenever she wished. But her shenanigans and grandiose ideas of her place in the world never bothered Jimmy; they just amused him.

Eileen expected to have the red carpet rolled out for her whenever she chose to appear unannounced at Priory Grove. I was in the kitchen when one of the children opened the door to Eileen soon after Paddy had begun working downstairs. As she was shown to the room, she eyed Paddy, who was seated in what she regarded as her spot. I entered the room as she was asking him what he did for a living. Paddy, who certainly must have known of Eileen's reputation among Jimmy's friends, gave an answer he probably calculated would divert her attention away from him.

'I'm a cobbler,' he replied.

'And where do you do your cobbling, Mr Kavanagh?'

'Oh, any place I can get work.'

'Mr Kavanagh, you can notice that I have very dainty feet. I would like you to make me a nice pair of dressy shoes, very small on the outside, but wide and comfortable on the inside.'

'Small on the outside and big and wide on the inside. That's a tall order.'

'You don't really want to work, do you? You're just looking for excuses.'

'I plead guilty!' exclaimed Paddy, anxious to get back to his writing, and wise enough not to be drawn into her drama. Paddy was well able to deal with the most difficult person I knew.

Jimmy loved the sea. He was a great swimmer and captain of a water polo team. He swam most mornings of the year, reciting Gerard Manley Hopkins' 'The Wreck of the Deutschland' to the rhythm of his Australian crawl – his idea of his morning prayers, no doubt![37] This regimen did not change with marriage, but I had more sense than to join him during his special brand of morning madness. As soon as each child reached what Jimmy considered 'swim-before-breakfast' age, he would bring them with him if the weather was good enough. By the time Paddy was staying with us, Jimmy was including our three older children in the morning swims. I was strongly disapproving. These swims wreaked havoc on an orderly morning pre-school schedule and resulted in disorderly, uncivilized breakfasts. My disapproval served only to give our children an added sense of delight in these treasured times with their father.

Jimmy got the kids up at six and they would get dressed in their swimming togs, pack their clothes and towels, all the while under strict instructions not to disturb me. Away they would drive to Seapoint. On their way home after the swim, they'd stop at the German Bakery in Blackrock, and Jimmy used to buy a freshly baked loaf of brown bread which, according to EllyMay, 'Daddy cracked over his knee and handed each a hunk through the car window, along with slices of hastily peeled oranges.' These they devoured with chattering teeth and great satisfaction. The German baker himself told me all about it with a big smile on his face.

Paddy was, of course, not included in these swims, and Jaja was too young. But it bothered my darling Jimmy that Paddy was missing out on these great times. He became determined to take Paddy for a swim, and he chose a Sunday – a day that would allow for a leisurely beach expedition.

So, on a sun-bright morning, Paddy and I found ourselves being persuaded seawards. It seemed that 'This day would never come again … and besides we surely did not want to spend the rest of our lives being sorry we had squandered the chance of precious time by the sea.'

Paddy, to give him his due, tried to explain that a day at the seaside was not his cup of tea, and that he did not swim.

'You don't have to. You can splash around like Betty.'

'Excuse me,' I defended. 'Maybe I won't win the Olympics, but I'm a good swimmer.'

'It's much easier than walking, Paddy. The water holds you up,' Margot told him.

Jimmy had been to the German Bakery and had the car packed with whole wheat bread cakes, Scotch eggs, Limerick ham, madeleine pastries, and lots of goodies, including apricots.

'I have writing to do. I haven't the time. I don't like crowds. I don't feel like meeting anyone. I want to stay here.' Paddy was resisting as best he could.

'That's exactly the point. You need to give yourself a break – a change of scene. The sea is so soul-satisfying, so embracing, so invigorating.'

Paddy opened the hall door and spat across the grass.

'Paddy is testing the wind. I think he's going to come, aren't you, Paddy?' Larry coaxed.

Paddy decided eventually that it was easier to go with the flow. 'All right, I'll come,' he relented.

'That's the spirit. Proust wrote only three words every few weeks,' said Jimmy as he closed his argument. 'Margot, Paddy is coming. Bring togs and plenty of towels.'

We drove some miles round the back of Bray Head, then up a hill and parked behind some houses.

'Now,' Jimmy instructed, 'if we go over there towards those fir trees, we'll find an opening. It leads to a lane that goes down to the sea.'

Paddy and the girls led the way. Larry and Jimmy were hauling the feast. My arms were full of swim gear. As I kept stumbling into huge green rhubarb leaves, clumps of lemon mint, gooseberry bushes, raspberry canes and the like, I realized that I was making my way through what must once have been the kitchen garden of a mansion, and that the lane we were headed towards was once the path from the mansion down to the sea. The children were delighted by the lane. The hazel bushes were arched over us making what Margot called a 'fairy-land summer house'.

EllyMay and Paddy were having a chat about the lovely job God had done on the lane. I paused, soaking in the fresh summer morning, the salty breeze that tossed the hazel bushes, the lush greenery of the ferns, ivy and sea peas. I reflected on how relaxed and happy Paddy always seemed to be when he was with the children. They accepted him as one of us, part of the family. After we had walked several hundred yards, we came out of the shadows of the lane into the blinding crystal splendour of the sea.

'Look, Jaja,' said Jimmy, 'we've come to the sea. Look at it, "Stretching like a sheet of silver all the way to Wales".' He was quoting a line from his play *Man Alive!*.

Larry and Margot were remarking that the stones were all the same slate-grey colour and had all been polished smooth by the sea.

'Why,' I said, surprised that I was surprised, 'we must be in Greystones.'

'Where's Paddy?' Jimmy asked as he was backing into the water with Jaja on his chest.

'He must be lost in the hazels,' I replied. But EllyMay informed us that he was talking to God, and Larry thought it likely that he was thinking up some new lines of poetry.

'As he would say himself, he is lost in the fog of enchantment,' Jimmy concluded.

Paddy came out from the shadows of the lane and peered into the shining distance, and then let his eyes roll along the beach.

'There's nobody here,' he sighed in great relief.

'Not a sinner in sight,' Larry assured him.

'Do you see that gaggle of geese heading towards the Sugar Loaf,' said Paddy with a chuckle, pointing to a formation of the birds flying to their summer home. 'There's not a sinner among them either.'

Paddy strolled slowly along the stone-studded beach laced with dried seaweed. A heron flew up from the reeds, her long legs trailing behind her.

'See,' I said. 'That is why we had to leave the dog at home. Many of the sea-birds nest in reeds.'

'Tigo doesn't bother birds,' said Larry, who always wanted to bring the dog wherever we went. 'Last one in is a rotten egg,' he called to his sisters as he hurried to get Jimmy's extra togs to Paddy.

'Mammy, you're going to be the rotten egg,' EllyMay called out with certainty.

It was my first swim of the season. I closed my eyes as I backed into the chilly sea. I was hesitating as I tried to convince myself that this was really what I wanted to do. EllyMay had her two eyes fastened on me, gleefully waiting to declare me a rotten egg. I could not chicken out now. I closed my eyes, fell back into the cold water and screamed my head off as I thrashed around.

'It's not too cold when you get used to it.' There behind me was Paddy, swimming on his back, both arms wheeling like oars on a rowboat.

'Look, Mama, Paddy has his own stroke,' Larry called to me.

'That's great,' I shivered. I bopped up and down a few times, and then made a dash for dry land, where Margot threw a dry towel over me.

'We're so proud of you, Mama. Now maybe you'll come with us every morning.'

'Maybe in July,' I said through chattering teeth.

I dressed as quickly as I could and set about getting the meal out of the crates and paper wrappings. I selected a dainty fish pie and bit into its crunchy crust. It was delicious, as were my samplings of the Scotch eggs with tasty sausage meat pressed around the hard-boiled egg centre. But, wonder of wonders, there in the corner of the wooden crate was a flask of hot tea. My husband was not too bad after all, and maybe the German baker knew a thing or two about good food. I poured myself a cup of steaming hot tea and drank with warm, satisfied sighs. What a brilliant idea to eat in peace before the children, ravenous after their swims, descended upon the feast. A madeleine and another cup of tea capped off a wonderful meal.

Feeling a little guilty for having fed myself first, I called out to the whole wide sea, 'A feast on the beach is such a great idea.'

I heard Jimmy translate my pronouncement for the kids. Having the best of French, Jimmy often spoke French to them. This was his way of helping them become familiar with the language and with proper pronunciation. I liked to stick to the Irish, so I called out the Irish translation to my swimming children.

Paddy came out of the water, beat himself with a towel, and stretched out on the sun-warmed stones.

'Oh,' he sighed, 'the utter contentment of having to do nothing.'

I placed a paper of buttered brown bread, a few Russian pies, and some Scotch eggs beside him and handed him a mug of tea.

Soon the other ravenous swimmers were munching contentedly.

'I've never had a madeleine,' said Paddy as he accepted one from Margot. 'I wondered about them when Proust was searching for his '*temps perdu*'. You remember how Swann was taken back to days gone by the aroma of the freshly baked madeleines.'

'Yes indeed,' I answered, 'nothing takes you back like the smell of home cooking.'

We made little boats from the paper wrappers, and the children named them. EllyMay's was called *Whirligig*,

Margot's *Wind-Song*, Larry's *Westward Ho* and *Flying Enterprise*. Jimmy and I joined in with *Over the Waves* and *The Jaja*. Paddy was really enjoying the fun and called his boat *Anna Liffey Plurabelle*. I gathered them on to the apron of my skirt and began the recitation of one of our most beloved poems, 'Sea-Fever', by John Masefield:

> I must go down to the seas again, to the lonely sea and
> the sky,
> And all I ask is a tall ship and a star to steer her by ...

Margot took over the recitation of the next lines, then Jimmy, then Larry, and then it was Paddy's turn and he came in with: 'And the flung spray and the blown spume, and the sea-gulls crying'.

Then we launched our ships. Over the waves they went. *Whirligig* spun round and round, much to EllyMay's delight. *Flying Enterprise* got shipwrecked on the grey stones of Greystones.

Eventually it was time to leave. At home the dog would need to be let out. Going through Bray, Paddy asked to stop the car. He went into a shop and returned with a bag of bull's-eyes, which he tossed to Larry to share with his sisters. He had a large box of cakes for me.

'Can you believe it! They had no gur cakes.[38] They never even heard of them!' he said in bewilderment.

'Paddy this is Bray, in County Wicklow, not Dublin,' Jimmy reminded him. 'Here they will have come up with some very fancy name for Gur cakes. You should hear Maureen Potter on the subject.'[39]

Our day at the seaside ended like all good school-boy essays: tired but happy we returned home.

I found Paddy's revelations about incidents from his past fascinating. He told me that during his first years in Dublin he had not found life easy. He wanted to write poetry, but he had to make a living. Jobs were scarce and, of course, he had no experience of city work. He was not sure what he could do to make money. He tried his hand at acting and, no doubt because his poetry had been published, he got taken on at the Abbey Theatre. Most of the actors were holding down other jobs and often turned up late for rehearsals. Paddy found the hanging around hard. It was even harder for him to take up the character of another person, so he drifted away from acting. He wrote the occasional article, but since he was not into the issues of the times, or at least the issues that would hold Dublin readers, he had a problem getting published.

At one point he had been hired as a public relations man to promote the spray-painting of haybarns. He wrote up a good rhyming sales pitch and practised delivering it with a certain amount of dash and rhythm. Given the static state of farming during those years, the job was not easy, but because Paddy was able to relate to country people, he had what could be described as success. His employers were very pleased. They were, he told me, the most decent and kind people you could ever hope to meet. Every Sunday morning, he would pick up his pay. The employers would be counting the week's takings up in a bedroom on the second floor above a shop on Stephen's Green. All the bank notes would be spread out on a multi-coloured eiderdown quilt and, after handing him his money, they'd say: 'Take a few notes there, whatever you need.' But he never did. Then they would all go off together for something to eat at McDaid's or some pub like it.

After some time, perhaps a year or so, Paddy realized that they were spray-painting over rust and the paint was flaking off with the rust. Paddy did not feel comfortable defrauding farmers in this way, so he took it up with his employers. They were taken aback. How could they go scraping off the rust first? It took too much time! Farmers wouldn't pay for the extra cost. No one would be able to make any money. Paddy's conscience got to him and he wrote an exposé and sent it to the *Farmers Journal*. It was published in the next edition and caused quite an uproar. That was how Paddy lost his job at a time when jobs were not easy to come by.

Worse still, some nights later, as he was making his way home, he was jumped on, rolled up in a quilt and tossed over Baggot Street Bridge into the canal.[40] It was a frosty night in late October, so the water was very cold. After he kicked his way clear of the quilt, he tried and tried but could not get up the steep canal bank. Even then, as he was giving up hope, he was trying to figure out who might have done this to him. He decided he couldn't blame them and said a prayer for whoever they were. He stretched out so that he was floating on his back and contemplated the stars. He tried to keep his toes and fingers moving. He floated against a beam of timber and was eventually able to use it to lever himself onto the bank, where he lay for some time. Then he crawled across the street and up the steps to the door of a house. He was too weak to get on his feet to use the knocker or doorbell, so he kicked the door every now and then with his water-filled boots. He shouted: 'Oh, for God's sake, someone open the door.'

Then someone was hurrying to the door and a loud voice was calling out an old Gaelic poem:

> *Ce he sin amiut?* (Who is that outside?)
> *Le facbar aer agut* (Shouting too loud)
> *Ag reaba me doras dunta?* (Banging at my closed door?)[41]

Paddy said that, amazingly, he recognized the poem and remembered the next line and managed to reply in Irish, '*Tá mé báite, fuar, fliuch*' (I'm drowned, cold, wet). But then he cried out, 'Oh, for God's sake, open the door. I've just climbed out of the canal. I need help.'

The door opened and a young woman stood in the doorway. Lights shone all around behind her. Was he hallucinating? Had he died, and had they sent a saint to greet him?

'Who are you? What are you doing here? Why are you lying on your back kicking my door?'

'My name is Patrick Kavanagh, and I need help.'

'The writer? I've heard of you. You're the poet. Should I call the police or an ambulance?'

'No, just let me warm up, and I'll be on my way.'

'I'll run a warm bath. Do you need help getting up? My father was here last month, and he left a huge robe, so you can get off those wet clothes. Come in. Let me help you.'

Paddy told me he thought the lady had an Australian accent. After the bath, he felt cosy and warm in a big black and gold robe. She made hot cocoa which he had with brown bread and cheese at the kitchen table. She told him she was from Australia and that her mother had died the previous year. She and her father had come to Ireland to recover. They had for years been talking about retiring to Ireland. They had travelled many places and her father had to go back home to take care of business, but she had decided to stay and do a course in Irish literature. She had a guest room and he was welcome to stay, but she would have to leave early in the morning. She would drop his clothes at the cleaners and pick them up on her way home.

Paddy slept like a log and found he had slept through the day when she came back with his clothes. She told him he could stay as long as he needed, and that there were cold meats in the fridge and plenty of bread. She had to go away for a few days and said to him: 'You say you are Patrick Kavanagh the writer. I've left pen and paper on the dining room table and there's lots of books.'

Paddy could not get over her kindness, and he went back to bed and slept until the next day. He wrote a poem that he had been mulling over in his head for some time. She came back on the Sunday, and they talked all afternoon. She was young and attractive but rather distant. She liked her own space and expected you to respect that. When Paddy got to this part of the story, his voice trailed off, perhaps lost in 'might-have-been's.

'Well,' I asked, 'what happened? Did ye fall in love or anything?'

'No,' he replied. 'She didn't anyway. I was trying to get something written. I wasn't thinking of anything like that, and she was a very classy person, very well educated. She wouldn't have been bothered with someone like me. When I got ready to leave, she said she'd take a walk with me, so we walked along the canal. I saw the quilt still in the canal. It was hard for me to admit to myself that I remembered it as the quilt on which the money was laid out upstairs from the shop on Stephen's Green. I told her about the spray-painting job and the article I had written for the *Farmers Journal,* how I believed they had every reason to be very angry with me. But I wasn't even sure it was them who threw me into the canal. We walked to McDaid's pub where my spray-painting friends were drinking. When they saw me, they shrank back into the darkness. Of course, they must have thought I was a ghost. "My friends are here. Maybe we should go somewhere else," I said to my lady friend. I was a bit sensitive about being seen with her, and women didn't go into pubs much.

'She said she would talk to them and she walked right over to them, that was the kind she was – direct. "Good evening, gentlemen, would you like to join us for a drink?"

One of them said, "That man you're with, who's he?"

"That's Patrick Kavanagh. Would you like to join us for a drink?"

"No, ma'am, thank you, not now. Some other time, maybe." '

And, according to Paddy, they scurried out of the pub.

'And what happened to the lovely lady?' I asked.

'We remained friends. I used to ring her up now and then. Once I helped her with something she was writing about Yeats. I haven't spoken to her in a long time. I did have her telephone number. I'm sure it is in that old address book.'

And I declare to goodness, didn't he get up off the couch and thumb through a tattered book, walk to the phone and dial her number. No, she said, she couldn't meet him that week, but she had to go to Wicklow the following weekend, would he like to come? Paddy did not hesitate. I heard him tell her '47 Priory Grove, Stillorgan.'

'You'll be here at 9:30 Friday morning? I'm staying with Jim O'Toole. Do you remember meeting him?'

A week later, on the dot of time, a sports car pulled up at Priory Grove and a woman got out.

'Paddy,' I called, 'she's arrived. Invite her in. I've got coffee on.'

Paddy was right: 'classy' was the best word for her, with her styled short-cropped hair, her fashionable suit and her wedge-heeled shoes. She was just lovely, relaxed and friendly. She laughed when she spoke of the night Paddy nearly kicked her door in. No, she had just had breakfast and did not need coffee. Would I like to go to Wicklow with them? Well, I would have loved to have gone, but my children would be back from school just after three. Besides, I was harbouring romantic ambitions for Paddy. After all, what was this elegant woman thinking, and what was Paddy thinking all spruced up and wearing his best suit? Maybe a romantic ending was not entirely out of the question.

'Paddy,' I said when he got home on Sunday evening, 'did she ask you to marry her?'

'No, but she did ask me to go to Australia with her.'

'That's almost the same thing.'

'She says she has lots of connections in the literary world.'

'You should think about it.'

'What about my writing? How could I just go off to Australia?'

'Put it in a big trunk and have it shipped. She seems to have plenty of money. She'll pay for it.'

'I think it would take me away from my work. I'm trying to type up a lot and put it together, and I think I would lose the mood and the feeling about things. And there's my health. Anyway, it would be unfair to her. She's very bright, she likes to move in society, to meet lots of people. I wouldn't be able for that. It's just not what I would like. I wouldn't be good at it ... and having to dress up. It's too exhausting even to think about. I know what London is like, but back then I enjoyed it – there was a lot of go-here and go-there. I met crowds of people, even famous people. But now I wouldn't have the time. Anyway, she's leaving fairly soon. Her dad is ill. I hope she meets up with someone with a lot of class.'

'Maybe she'll come back,' I said.

'I asked her that, and she said it wasn't likely.'

It crossed my mind that if he had made a definite proposal of marriage, she might have considered it. But he had evidently decided that she was way beyond his reach.

The very next morning, who walked in but my Uncle Bob. He was a doctor, had a practice in Matlock, and lived in Ripley, Derbyshire. He had come over on the ferry with his car, and had driven from the ferry to my door, stopping only to pick up bacon, sausages, and several kinds of bread in Blackrock. Six foot two, Uncle Bob was casual, easy-going, and a favourite with everyone. He got along especially well with Jimmy. We were in the kitchen, frying-pans were on, rashers sizzling, sausages rolling, eggs turning, bread toasting, all of us talking together.

'You usually come for Horse Show week in August. How come you're over now?' Jimmy asked.

'Well, I've a man to look up – I should say find. I really don't know where to look for him. Then I'll be heading to Clare, maybe Monaghan, and of course to see the nuns Josie and Mary in Wexford. That is if I find my man. I promised these two ladies in Matlock that I'd look for him and with luck I'll find him.'

'What two ladies?' I asked. Uncle Bob was a widower, so I liked to tease him. 'One lady would be more to the point.'

'No, no! Don't be getting notions! Anyway, one is a nun and the other my very competent assistant. When my partner, Dr Kelly, retired a few years ago, I thought I'd cut down and not take on so many patients. But patients kept on coming, so I advertised for a nurse, and a nurse applied who had been a theatre nurse in one of the big London hospitals for some years. She wrote that she was looking for something less demanding where she'd meet more people and get back to living in the country. Then at the end of her letter she mentioned she had a sister, a nun in a convent in Matlock, so she believed the job with me might suit her well. I thought she might just fit the bill, so I wrote her, suggesting she come see her sister, spend some time in my surgery, and if she were happy with the place, she might think of staying. Well, she's a top-notcher, very competent, very sound, very knowledgeable and helpful, so I hired her. Then one evening when she and her sister, the nun, were over for tea, they mentioned they had a brother a poet. Well, I said my dad was a poet, so next thing I knew I was reading their brother's poetry and found I was inviting him up from London to see them.[42] He came. We got along fine. He spent most of his time with his sisters, sight-seeing. One day I took him down a coal-mine where I had to treat an injured man. Then we went to the Doncaster races together. He introduced me to Elizabeth Arden, the cosmetics lady. Macmillan is his publisher. I must find him. His name is—'

'Patrick Kavanagh,' Jimmy cut in. 'I'll find him for you. He's above in bed!'

'Above in bed? You're joking me! How could he be above in bed? Here?'

'Why don't you go up and see for yourself. He must be about up now.'

Uncle Bob dashed up the stairs and between the hopping and the jumping, the chattering and the contradicting, Paddy wanted to know where I'd found Dr Robert Ryan of Ripley and Uncle Bob wanted to know where I'd found Paddy. In no time at all they had decided to go to Inniskeen and were all climbing into Uncle Bob's car – Jimmy deciding to take the day off and me regretting I could not go. There was little Jacqueline, and the others would be back from school at 3:30.

'Of course you're coming,' Paddy said, and that decided me. I now had an invitation to the Kavanagh home. I ran into Mrs Meredith, our neighbour, and explained the situation.

'Oh,' she said, 'I'll keep an eye out for them. They can play with my boys in the back garden, and don't worry.'

I grabbed my toddler and jumped in the car. Uncle Bob was driving. Jimmy had put Paddy in beside him. Uncle Bob had lots of comments as we drove through Dublin. After all, he had gone to college there. But as we were getting nearer to Kavanagh country, Paddy took over. He had walked from Inniskeen to Dublin several times, he told us, and it was no short walk. He knew every twist and turn in the road, every stick and stone, every farm and fence, every town and village. When we got to Inniskeen he was alive with memories of happenings, people and places. The Caseys lived up that road, the Maguires had a shop down that lane that sold absolutely everything. He jumped out of the car, rushed up the street and bought the local newspaper, *The Anglo-Celt*. He was in tip-top form, delighted with life. He turned to walk back, delight and pleasure at the excitement of being himself, the sheer joy of living, of being there. The paper was flapping in his left hand. His right hand came to steady it so he could read the front page.

'Christ Almighty! How can this have happened?' His chin fell. His whole countenance changed to dismay and confusion.

'What is it, Paddy?' Jim was out of the car.

'It's the school,' Paddy said. 'The old school has burned down, and it's still on fire.'

'No!' a passerby said, 'it's under control. They think no one was lost or hurt. It's still smoking though.'

'Get in,' Uncle Bob called. 'Where's the school? We'll drive to it.'

We drove into the school yard. There were still firemen around and there was still a little smoke from the school.

Paddy walked over to what was left of the school, his shoulders drooping.

'All the children safe?' he asked.

'Oh yes, sir,' the fireman answered him. 'The fire started during the early morning; nobody was inside. We went through it. Nobody lost, thanks be to God.'

'The principal saved some of the furniture,' a second fireman said. Paddy ambled over and opened two old oak desks. His hands went lovingly over them. He returned to us very upset.

'That young principal saved all the new desks. They're very light, made of that cheap pine, and they aren't worth a 'coldoy'.[43] If they'd saved my desk, they could have built a new school in every parish in the county when they auctioned it off.'

'Paddy,' I said, 'they saved a couple of the old oak desks. Maybe one of those could have been yours.'

'No,' he said. 'I looked. I had carved "P.K." on the inside with my penknife.' He laid his hand on the yard wall and his head down against a tree. No one spoke for the next five minutes. Paddy's grief was what I brought away most from that day.

'He seems completely knocked out,' Uncle Bob said.

'I think he's saying the De Profundis,' Jimmy said. 'I don't know if it's for the school, the desk, or for himself.'

'Oh, it's just for times gone by,' I said. But I, too, wondered. As well as for the school and himself, was he also grieving the loss to the future children of Inniskeen?

'I'll see if I can get him a cup of coffee or a beer or something. Maybe a brandy,' said Uncle Bob and walked up the road. We waited another few minutes. Then Jim went to talk to Paddy, and they returned slowly to the car. Paddy rang his sister from a telephone booth. Uncle Bob came back with what looked like a double brandy which Paddy tossed back.

Shortly after, we arrived at the Kavanagh homestead, just outside the village. Having read *Tarry Flynn*, I might have expected a neglected place, but it was a fine, well-kept farmhouse, a real home with a hedge and several flowerbeds in the garden. Paddy's sister Bridie was at the door. She gave him a great welcome. He turned and introduced me, then Jim and Uncle Bob, who gave her some parcels from the two sisters in England. He also brought in a box of chocolates, biscuits and a few bottles of wine which he presented to Bridie.

'We'll give you two some time to catch up,' said Uncle Bob to Paddy and his sister.

'I've the kettle on, so don't go far,' Bridie called after us.

We took a walk by the poplar trees. My little Jaja had woken up so I let her walk on the pathway through the grass. Jimmy and Bob followed me. We went to the famous Haggard Gate and down the field.[44]

> And then I came to the haggard gate,
> And I knew as I entered that I had come
> Through fields that were part of no earthly estate.

Jaja ran to Jimmy and he swung the child up onto his shoulders. 'I've no pitchfork on my shoulder, but I have my Jacqueline,' he sang to the child, modifying words from Paddy's poem 'A Reverie of Poor Piers' to the situation at hand. 'Less for ease than for devilment,' Jimmy continued in the same vein.

The day had brightened up, but we turned back. When we reached the house, there was a lovely meal laid out on the kitchen table. I fed my little girl from my plate. Uncle Bob did most of the talking, all about the two girls in Matlock.

'They brought Ireland in the door to me,' he told us all. Then he stood up and said, 'I think this is an occasion for a toast, or indeed, many toasts. First, to Bridie for inviting us into her lovely home. Then here's to Patrick Kavanagh and myself, because I have found him, and he is in wonderful good health. And to Betty and Jimmy, who have many stories to tell us later.'

After we had eaten, Paddy and Jimmy went upstairs. Paddy had a trunk of papers under his desk he wanted to go through. I sat by the fire with my baby. Someone came to the door about cattle. Paddy's sister threw a coat on her shoulders and went out. Uncle Bob went up the stairs to join Paddy and Jimmy, and when he came back down with Jimmy, they each had an armful of papers which they carried out to the car. They decided to take a walk together and took Jaja with them. When Paddy finally came downstairs, he was also carrying papers.

He said, 'I think I will be back to help Bridie with a few things, but I'm going to take a quick walk to the cut-away bog. Would you like to come with me?'

'Oh, I'd love that, I'll put on my coat.'

We walked down through the grassy fields.

'Paddy,' I said, 'you seem to be back to yourself.'

'Yes,' he replied, 'I feel good, like I used to. It was your friendly advice, Betty, that helped me realize that it was up to myself to find the man I was. Your children helped restore me to myself.'

We came to the bog.

'So here we are. We'll say our poem, which I dedicate to your children. I will bring them here some day to recite it,' and together we recited his poem 'The One':

Green, blue, yellow and red —
God is down in the swamps and marshes
Sensational as April and almost incred-
    ible the flowering of our catharsis.
A humble scene in a backward place
Where no one important ever looked;
The raving flowers looked up in the face
Of the One and the Endless, the Mind that has baulked
The profoundest of mortals. A primrose, a violet,
A violent wild iris – but mostly anonymous performers
Yet an important occasion as the Muse at her toilet
Prepared to inform the local farmers
That beautiful, beautiful, beautiful God
Was breathing His love by a cut-away bog.[45]

We left for home by four-thirty, Paddy promising to keep in touch with Bridie. Uncle Bob and Paddy chatted away on the way back, Jimmy leaning forward and adding a little every now and then. The conversations were wide-ranging, covering the land, religion, the Church and its missteps, traditions, families, customs and culture, the place of poetry in education, and, of course, literature – James Joyce, Liam O'Flaherty, and Paddy's *The Great Hunger*.

'I'm sorry I wrote it,' Paddy said,

'Someone had to write it. The truth isn't easy,' Uncle Bob replied.

I sat back, thinking to myself, how is it these three men get along so well? Why is there so much empathy between them? Is it The Land? Divine Influence? Farming? They spoke so easily to one another. And as for Paddy, where was all his crustiness gone? This was a different Patrick Kavanagh, a relaxed, good-humoured, well-spoken man, really enjoying himself and those around him. Had he found himself? Was that what he meant when he said to me, 'Your children helped restore me to myself'?

Paddy Kavanagh, I said silently to myself, you are a man well worth finding and restoring. So welcome back.

A road, a mile of kingdom. I am king
Of banks and stones and every blooming thing.[46]

Patrick Kavanagh at Priory Grove

MARGOT O'TOOLE[1]

The addition of a poet to our household did not seem out of the ordinary to us. It was not uncharacteristic of my parents to help Patrick Kavanagh; our home was a welcoming place for those in need of generous hearts. As children, we were accustomed to people who stayed a while and became enveloped in our family life. We often had extra guests around the table at mealtimes, and we took it for granted that anyone staying with us would join us on family outings.

The descriptions in my mother's manuscript of my father's sweeping insistence that Paddy would come to the Punchestown Races and the day we spent at the seaside in Greystones are just as I remember them. Each of my siblings has memories of other excursions which are not described by my mother: for example, he came with us for a hike on the Sugarloaf Mountain in County Wicklow, to an art exhibition near the Featherbed Forest, overlooking Dublin, and to Bulloch Harbour in Dalkey, County Dublin, where we bought fish from a fisherman. My father's exuberance enveloped those around him and swept them along. Patrick Kavanagh, often portrayed in years since then as a curmudgeon, joined right in.

It was not only house guests who were invited to join us on family outings. My parents believed in sharing good times as widely as possible. When dad took us anywhere for fun – to the beach, a movie, a museum, on a hike – he would bring along any other relative or neighbourhood child who could get permission to come with us. As one of my cousins said to me recently: 'I remember him as the person who never left any of us behind.' My father's car would have reminded you of those clown cars, loaded with an impossibly large number of passengers. Once, when we were travelling on a country road in west Clare, we passed a man on foot. Dad, as was second nature to him, stopped to offer a ride. The bewildered man pointed out that the car was packed to the brim with us and our cousins and he could not fit into it. Dad directed him to stand on the running board, the bundle he was carrying was passed in to me, and I held it on my lap as I sat on someone else's lap. Front and back car windows were rolled down so our new passenger could keep a secure grip on the frame of the car as we proceeded slowly along the bumpy road.

Paddy enjoyed the company of children. He showed an interest in us, he took part in our fun, and he was supportive. We shared with him what his poems asked children to share with him – the 'meadow ways' of our innocence and laughter.

Our experience with Paddy was similar to Kieran Markey's, Paddy's nephew, who recalled Paddy taking him out to kick football: they played for a while but then his uncle said, 'Go and play on your own, I want to do some dramin' (dreaming) for myself.' He would stand gazing over the fields and let the child play on his own.[2] Yet his way with children has not, in my opinion, received the attention it deserves. Perhaps this is because Paddy's nephew John Quinn has reported that Paddy paid no attention to him as a child when he and the poet were staying with his sister, Annie, at her home in Longford town in 1955.[3] However, Paddy was at that time recovering from having a lung removed and was undoubtedly even more ill than he was when he arrived in our home some years later. Paddy's interactions with us mirrored the attitudes to children expressed in his poetry. In his 1953 ballad, 'If Ever You Go to Dublin Town', he describes himself 'Playing through the railings with little children/ Whose children have long since died.'[4] There seems to have been a healing and restorative dimension for him in the company of children. Little wonder then that in his poem 'Advent' he openly coveted 'the luxury/ Of a child's soul' as essential to his poetic vision.[5]

Poetry was at the core of my parents' friendship with Paddy. In our home, poems were part of daily life. They were stored in memory so that we could call upon them when needed – needed that is to put experience into the inspirational context of shared humanity; to instil an understanding of our culture; to reveal how language can express ideas and emotions. Each of us learned a different set of poems. It was only after I became an adult that I realized each list must have been selected based on our individual personalities. For the most part, all of us knew the poems from all the lists because we would hear them repeatedly recited. But there was never any doubt about which of us could claim the special connection to a given poem.

For instance, whenever my little sister EllyMay started to cry, my father would grab a small cloth – a handkerchief, a table napkin, whatever was closest at hand – and announce that he was about to perform a 'great magic trick'. He would then use the cloth to shield EllyMay's face from his 'audience' and begin to recite. Often, but not always, he chose 'Kubla Khan' by Samuel Taylor Coleridge because the words at the beginning sounded magical to us:

> In Xanadu did Kubla Khan
> A stately pleasure-dome decree

Then, with a magician's flourish, he would whip away the cloth to reveal the laughing face of EllyMay. Transforming an upset child into a child who was laughing uncontrollably, with the tears still wet on her face, was a magic trick that never failed.

As I recall, my father dealt with my own displays of upset in private, perhaps because I was more private about them, or perhaps because I am failing to remember incidents that occurred when I was very young. He had a single, special poem for me. He would stand squarely, reach his arched arms towards me in a ballet-like pose, and melodiously recite Gerard Manley Hopkins' 'Spring and Fall', emphasizing the syllables as Hopkins did:

Márgarét, áre you gríeving
Over Goldengrove unleaving?
Leáves like the things of man, you
With your fresh thoughts care for, can you?

The brew of emotions he would stir up with this performance was complicated. This large and loving person focusing intensely on me always seemed to distract me from whatever had saddened me. Often at the start of the recitation, I would feel annoyed that my right to be appropriately upset was not being validated. His recitation would stop when I smiled at him. Sometimes he did not get that smile until near the end of the poem. But I *would* smile. How could I deny him the pleasure of having his charm work on me?

My father recited many other poems to me, of course. I remember sitting as a small child in the lap of a big and strong man and, in what may seem like an unfathomable paradox, I would get the sensation of being big too. Looking back now at this sense of small-child 'bigness', I suppose the world of literature that he was laying out before me made me feel like I had a place in the world. One day as I scrambled to get up on his lap, I said to him, 'I feel so big in your arms.' The pleasure and pride he took in recounting this early interaction between us never diminished.

Much of our education at home happened through poetry. My mother's sister, Auntie Kitty, told the story that once upon a time, returning from a few years of working in the USA, she asked me to say a poem for her. I was what she described as 'a tiny bit of a thing,' and so she was expecting a nursery rhyme. Instead I subjected her to a full-length recitation of

'The Lady of Shalott' by Tennyson, all 171 lines of it. Some, I am sure, would say that teaching this long poem to a very young child was silly. But with the mastery of that poem came a broadened vocabulary, an awareness of the stories of Camelot and the outfitting of knights, and an appreciation of how words could be strung together beautifully. My brother Larry did something similar: he recited the entire 143 lines of 'Lepanto' by G.K. Chesterton on stage at school when he was about eight. Both he and I learned some history from it. My sister Jaja has especially tender memories of reciting Tennyson's 'Maud' and T.S. Eliot's 'The Love Song of J. Alfred Prufrock' with my father.

My father's cousin Michael Hayes has told me that my father, upon returning to their shared room the evening he had met my mother, recounted how he had recited poetry to her. It came as no surprise to me that poetry had helped dad win my mom's heart. From the very beginning, it was part of the glue that held them together. My mother recites poetry honed to the situation at hand — I use the present tense because she is still doing it as I write this in October 2019. Her father also loved to tell us stories, with favourites retold many times. Sometimes his storytelling was in the form of epic poems recited from memory. He was very interested in the USA and was a great admirer of Longfellow. His recitations of Longfellow's 'The Slave's Dream' made a big impression on me, and because he often recited 'The Midnight Ride of Paul Revere', I arrived as an Irish girl in my American History class in Massachusetts knowing as much as, if not more than, my classmates did about their local hero.

*James Davitt Bermingham
O'Toole and Elizabeth Ryan
on their wedding day in
St John's Church, Cratloe,
County Clare, 27 August 1949.*

*Elizabeth O'Toole's daughter Margot at the unveiling of Henry Moore's
sculpture* Knife Edge *in honour of W.B. Yeats in St Stephen's Green, Dublin,
in 1967; from left, the architect Michael Scott, an unidentified man, Henry
Moore, the playwright Lennox Robinson, and the sculptor F.E. McWilliam.*

Patrick Kavanagh in the garden of Priory Grove, Stillorgan. Elizabeth O'Toole is on the left, obscuring her nephew Robert Ryan who is holding up a ball with Larry O'Toole. In front of him, clockwise, are Margot O'Toole and two cousins, Ann and Mary Clare Harvey, Jaqueline (JaJa) O'Toole and EllyMay O'Toole on Kavanagh's right. The photo was probably taken in the spring of 1961.

EllyMay O'Toole and Patrick Kavanagh. The flowers and the car suggest the photograph was taken by her father or mother on one of the many occasions Kavanagh joined the family on days out in the country.

Guthán
Oifig na dTicéad   44505
Oifig an Rúnaí   45412

AMHARCLANN NA MAINISTREACH

BLEÁ CLIATH, C.8. ABBEY THEATRE, DUBLIN.

Dáta 3rd., November, 1958.

Stiurthóirí: LEAMHNACH ROBASTÚN, EARNAN DE BLAGHD,
ROIBEARD Ó FARACHAIN, SÉAMUS DE BHILMOT
Bainisteoir Stiurtha: EARNAN DE BLAGHD
Rúnaí: ERIC GORMAN

J. D. B. O'Toole, Esq.,
47, Priory Grove,
Stillorgan,
DUBLIN.

Dear Mr. O'Toole,

It is an old saying that too many cooks spoil the broth and I am afraid that too much advice from different angles has been bad for the re-writing of MAN ALIVE! I personally agree with those who having read the last version say that the change has been very much for the worse.

If it had been possible to produce MAN ALIVE in its or form with everybody fully convinced that it was a slashing attack on the E.S.B. and that individuals who could be identified by those in the know (and who would soon have bee identified by rumour) were being deliberately pilloried, the play would have excited pretty wide interest. Seeing it in that form nobody would have minded its exaggeration a one-sidedness. It would have been looked upon as a lampoo and up to a certain extent the more unfair it was the more people would have liked it.

,   Danger of libel actions as well as general Abbey polic; which forbids attacks on individuals or specific institutio: necessitated the substitution of some non-existent body for

Public Office. It is nicely written but I feel tl

Ernest Blythe's letter rejecting James O'Toole's play Man Alive!. *Note that the letterhead does not name the Abbey Theatre, and that the typist has deleted the name of the recently deceased member of the Board, Leamnach Robastún (Lennox Robinson).*

Man alive!

I would like S.P. to know I took his criticisms of the manuscript of "Man Alive!" very much to heart, e.g:

1.—Characterisation which asks an audience to take too much on trust. As staged, references by one character about another are kept to the minimum required to push the plot along.

2.—"The inconsequential nature of much of the plot." Side plots: e.g., Ring-Helen, Joan Young-Hannigan, incidental nepotism, etc., etc., have been cut out.

3.—"The way it states its theme." A very important point. Here, S.P. was dead right. Last August, Father Aidan and O'Malley just agreed with each other. Now they confront each other in a dramatic situation, where Father Aidan reminds O'Malley that his resolution to stay should take account of the fact that his wife had taken no vow of poverty. The searching exchange between them brings out the very moment in time when Father Aidan himself planted the living seed of Christian personality in O'Malley and so cut him loose to sink or swim in the here-and-now as only he can choose.

Finally, Godfrey Quigley has not doctored Man Alive!, but Jim Fitzgerald has. He has cut the play by a third or more. I think Jim and Godfrey are in the same class, as directors.

Is it possible that S.P. has carried over subconsciously his memory of the "raw material"?

James O'Toole
Stillorgan.

" Shatteringly authentic executive types . . . in a concern where the zombies have taken over."

JOHN JORDAN in *Hibernia*

"Beyond any question a most unusual comedy . . . a powerful comedy. Mr. O'Toole is a dramatist of imaginative power and very considerable writing ability."

TOM COLLINS in *Dublin Opinion*

"*Man Alive* is the greatest Catholic play which Dublin has had the opportunity of seeing in two generations . . . Mr. O'Toole is a modern Don Quixote . . . tilting at very real windmills of bureaucracy, dishonesty and materialistic society."

SEAMUS G. O'KELLY in *The Standard*

"Dramatic excitement . . . hard, economical, urgent . . . high spirited chaos . . . recalling Elmer Rice and the Marx Brothers . . . tremendous integrity . . . a strange play, but one very much alive."

A. R. in *The Irish Times*

"Originality and power . . . etched in acid."

R. M. F. in *The Evening Mail*

12/6

Left: *Jim O'Toole's response, on 27 January 1961, to the* Evening Press *review of* Man Alive! *reveals that the director, Jim Fitzgerald, had cut the play by one third.* Right: *Quotes praising* Man Alive! *on the flyleaf of the Allen Figgis edition of the play published in 1963.*

[v]

*A publicity photo of
Jim O'Toole for his play*
Man Alive!.

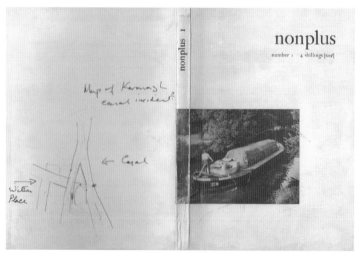

Nonplus, *the literary magazine edited by Patricia Avis, published in
October 1959. For an unknown reason, this copy, owned and annotated by
the editor Brian Lynch, has a map on the back cover showing the Grand
Canal into which Patrick Kavanagh was thrown that month, and the
location of Avis's house on Wilton Terrace where he sought refuge.*

Patricia Avis, known as Patricia Strang when she was married to Professor Colin Strang, and as Patsy Murphy when she was married to the poet Richard Murphy.

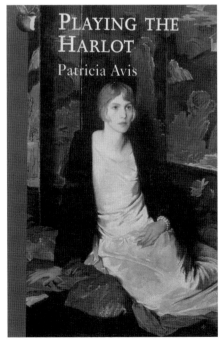

The cover of the Virago Press edition of Patricia Avis's novel Playing the Harlot, *published posthumously in 1996.*

Elizabeth O'Toole celebrating her ninety-fifth birthday with children, grandchildren and great-grandchildren on the beach at Newport, Rhode Island, in 2019. Her son Larry (Laurence Paul Claudel) is on the extreme right. Her daughters, Margot, EllyMay, and Jacqueline (JaJa), are respectively first, third and fourth on the left.

Elizabeth O'Toole, in her ninety-seventh year, signing the contract for A Poet in the House *in March 2021.*

As a child, I enjoyed Paddy's company and his poems. I don't remember knowing that Paddy was famous – that he had already gained wide acclaim as among the greatest poets of the English language. I only remember thinking of him as our friend, and that my parents believed him to be a very important poet. I occasionally organized papers for Paddy. I was, he said, not a 'chatterbox'. While I busied myself, he would spend a lot of time staring out the window with a pen or pencil in his hand. There was a fair bit of grunting and spitting as he did this. He would scratch, or seemed to scratch, at the page, and at times seemed to start anew. It was not unusual to see very little movement, and seemingly very little progress, but sometimes he would bestir himself and start banging away at his typewriter. I brought him a cup of tea with milk and sugar whenever he asked for one. He would add a small amount of whiskey from a very small bottle, a naggin.

Even as a child, it was obvious to me that Paddy was engaged in a serious endeavour. My parents shared with him the conviction that poetry was important at an earthy, daily-life level; that it was not a luxury but a necessity. From the perspective of poetry as luxury, we can sometimes take great pride in our poets and yet expect them to write without having a basic income. This disrespectful and dismissive attitude to the financial challenges of being a poet was evident in the anonymously sourced and anonymously authored disparaging profile of Paddy that appeared in *The Leader* magazine in October 1952. Moreover, in her biography of Paddy, Antoinette Quinn vitiates the hurt caused to Paddy by that with the assertion that he perceived it as a money-making opportunity. She describes his reaction as 'deeply wounded and offended, yet not so distraught that he did not immediately perceive the potential silver lining attaching to this particular cloud. If the "Profile" proved libellous, it could prove a nice little earner.'[6]

My parents regarded Paddy's poetry as essential, especially to Irish people. My father, as an engineer and journalist, and my mother, as a home economist and teacher, were passionately committed to their professions and believed them to be of the utmost importance. In their eyes, the writing of poetry was no less so. Their friendship was cemented by this shared belief. My dad himself wrote poems occasionally. Most often, however, his focus was on translation. He grew up speaking French and Chinese and he was fluent in German, so he was well-positioned to give English speakers access to work he believed to be important and influential. I remember in particular 'The Ballad of the Children's Shoes', which he translated from a poem in German by Alma Holgersen.[7]

My father had an extraordinary personality and personal history. He was born in Shanghai and lived in the Shanghai International Concession until he was almost nineteen years old. (The settlement was established in the mid-nineteenth century by international treaty, and at the time of my father's birth, 1915, it was administered by Britain and the United States.) Like all Irish people born before independence, my father started life as a British subject, but he grew up with neighbours, friends, classmates and co-workers who were Chinese, French, American, Russian, Jewish, and British. The social diversity of his childhood resulted in a very broad-minded person with great knowledge of, appreciation for, and sensitivity towards, other cultures.

His mother, who had been a teacher in Ireland before her marriage in 1911, lectured in the French College and became principal of the Jewish School in Shanghai. She was the daughter of Thomas Bermingham, an activist in the Land League movement in County Clare. My father's middle name, Davitt, honoured Michael Davitt, the movement's leader. My grandfather also came from a family with a history of defiance of British authority in Ireland. As he rose through the ranks of the police in Shanghai, eventually achieving the rank of Commissioner, he took many opportunities to demonstrate his independence from British policy and social conventions. One often-repeated anecdote was that he very publicly welcomed, and threw a large international banquet for, an Australian visitor to Shanghai who had shortly before been prevented by British authorities from setting foot on Irish soil.

My dad attended French-speaking schools and was fluent in French. Very outgoing by nature, he made friends with Chinese boys, both the sons of labourers and of powerful people. All the members of the O'Toole family socialized with Chinese people, and all spoke some Mandarin. My grandfather spoke it well. However, very few of the people living in the International Concession spoke any Chinese dialect. Dad spoke with his Chinese friends in the dialect of Shanghai.

When we were growing up, dad would tell us of his visits to the homes of his Chinese friends, describing both the poverty and opulence he witnessed. He spoke about how young and small some of his Chinese friends were when they began working as rickshaw pullers, and about the brilliance of some of his Chinese classmates. With great amusement he recounted the consternation he caused when one of his pals agreed to give him a turn pulling a rickshaw – socializing with rickshaw pullers was apparently a serious social transgression; alarmed and vociferous complaints were made to his parents.

My father was an extraordinarily successful student. At the age of fourteen, he sat for the London University Matriculation exam and the Cambridge University Leaving Certificate. He won an open scholarship for physics and mathematics. He also received awards for essay writing. When he was sixteen, he enrolled in the Université l'Aurore, the French Jesuit University in Shanghai, and studied pure mathematics, kinetics, physics, organic and inorganic chemistry, and moral philosophy.[8] In December 1933, at the age of eighteen, he sat the exam for the Peace Memorial Scholarship, a highly competitive and prestigious scholarship awarded to two males per year. In March 1934 he was awarded that scholarship. In December 1933, while still studying mathematics at the university, he signed on as a proofreader at the *North China Daily News*, an English-language newspaper in Shanghai known as the most influential foreign newspaper of its time. He was quickly promoted to junior sub-editor, and by the summer of 1934 he had been assigned to prepare for publication a geography of China, province by province.

But later that year, grandfather, then aged fifty-five, decided to go back to Ireland, largely because Shanghai had become politically unstable. Chiang Kai-shek was purging the allies who had helped him gain control of the newly reunified China. My grandmother told me that they returned to Ireland due to what was perceived to be an impending Japanese invasion – the Japanese had already bombed Shanghai in 1932. The O'Tooles had correctly perceived the threat: Japan did invade, in 1937. Europeans living in Shanghai were arrested and imprisoned in internment camps. The native Chinese suffered much worse fates.

My father left Aurora University without having obtained his degree. Although he was clearly a brilliant student, he took pains to explain that he was not among the top three in his class: they were Chinese. One day they were arrested as part of Chiang Kai-shek's ongoing consolidation of power. My father believed they were executed. This tragedy forced him to accept what his parents had concluded: Shanghai had become too dangerous.

By October 1934, my father had enrolled on his open Peace Memorial Scholarship as a second-year student at University College Dublin. By any measure he excelled in UCD. He won gold and silver medals for Oratory and Impromptu Debate; served as President of the Student Representative Council for two years and was managing editor of the monthly college magazine. He was also an excellent athlete, captaining the swimming team, playing water polo and rugby, and throwing the discus. By the autumn of 1938, he had obtained degrees in Mechanical and Electrical Engineering and in Geology. We have a letter signed by A.W. Conway, Acting President of the college, recording that dad had a '1st in Science 1938'.

Upon graduation, dad secured a position with a world-renowned firm, Siemens-Schuckert, in Berlin. According to his passport, he arrived in Germany on 26 February 1939 and by May had been assigned to the company's headquarters in Berlin. He began working on the design of a hydroelectric plant in Waag, Czechoslavakia.[9] Less than four months later, on 31 August, the Nazis invaded Poland. Later that week, the *Irish Press* reported that my father's parents had lost contact with him.

It is now known that at this time the Germans had formed an alliance with Seán Russell, Chief of Staff of the IRA.[10] Many in the IRA rejected the alliance with the Nazis, and there were deep splits within the organization. In Germany, attempts were made to recruit Irish people. Not surprisingly, my father became a target of this recruiting campaign. If he did not immediately understand that the Nazis never took 'no' for an answer, a person he described to us only as 'a decent German chap' warned him that he was in danger and should flee immediately. He was not able to leave, however, because he had lost his Irish passport. He went into hiding for the next four months, a time during which his parents were spreading the word that he had gone missing in Berlin. My father kept secret for the rest of his life the identities of those who had sheltered and helped him during those months.

By the end of September, the Irish Legation in Berlin had issued a replacement passport. By the end of December, a visa to enter Belgium had been issued to him by the Belgian Embassy. Two days later he left Germany. On 3 January 1940 he travelled by boat from Ostend in Belgium to Folkestone in England, and from there on to London where he had a very good friend. On 7 January, he travelled from Holyhead, Wales to Dublin.[11]

Upon his return, my father shared with the Irish government what he had gleaned from the efforts of the Germans to recruit him, an action that, according to his close friend Michael Hayes, may have exposed him to hostility from the IRA. At this time the alliance with the Nazis was at a crucial stage: in the summer of 1940, a German submarine carrying IRA Chief of Staff Seán Russell sailed close to County Galway, but he became ill, died on board and was buried at sea. The mission was aborted. How much my father knew of all this is not known, but after he had communicated with the Irish government a Garda Síochána detail kept watch on his parents' home, where he was staying, until the end of the war.[12]

Michael Hayes's information that my dad had carried information from Germany, first to a friend in London and then to the Irish government, fits well with a mysterious experience I had in 1964 when my father took me with him on a trip to London. One evening we went to dinner at the home of a very good friend from his days at UCD. Upon arrival we were greeted by a small group of English people who spent the evening in high spirits toasting James Davitt Bermingham O'Toole for the important role he had played in England's 'most dark and dangerous' days. My father, who had been expecting a quiet dinner with an old pal, remained uncharacteristically subdued throughout the evening. Later I tried to draw him out about the important role the English people said he had played during the war, but he just told me that little attention should be paid to men with 'drink taken'.

At the end of 1940 my father passed the examination for another degree from UCD, this time in Technology, with a major in 'Advanced Theory in High Voltage Transmission'. In March 1941 he passed the Associated Membership Examination of the Institute of Mechanical Engineers and was elected Associate Member of the Institution of Civil Engineers (London) in 1945. Between 1941 and 1945, he worked as an engineer in various places, including the Great Northern Railroad Co. (Ireland); as Assistant Engineer for Roads and Buildings in County Clare; as a consultant for a group of Irish manufacturing firms; and as a lecturer at the College of Technology in Bolton Street, Dublin. He played as a forward for Bective Rangers Rugby Club, and in 1944 they won the Metropolitan Cup.[13] When the war ended, he worked with British Acheson Electrodes in Sheffield; with Gordon Laycock engineering in Leeds; and as a Senior Lecturer at the College of Technology in Rotherham. A letter of recommendation from the last institute praises his wide background, experience, and teaching skills. It also states: 'Mr O'Toole is a good "Rugger" player and plays regularly for the Rotherham First Fifteen.'

In November 1948 my father, who was engaged to marry my mother at the time, accepted a position with the Electricity Supply Board (ESB). At first things progressed satisfactorily, despite a motorcycle accident that left him badly injured on Christmas Day, 1948. Between 1948 and March 1954 he worked on rural electrification, driving from place to place in his beloved Riley car. He was in his element working from local ESB district headquarters with local government authorities and farmers. In trips I have taken back to Ireland as an adult, I have met people who remembered him with fondness, appreciation and nostalgia. During these years he and my mother got married (in August 1949); they bought 47 Priory Grove, Stillorgan; Larry was born in December 1950; and I was born in June 1952.

But this happy period came to an end. On 20 March 1954 the following item appeared in *The Nationalist and Leinster Times*: 'Regret is caused by the announcement of the transfer to Dublin of Mr James D.B. O'Toole, electrical engineer, who has been attached to the ESB district headquarters here since October. A talented actor, Mr O'Toole will be remembered in Portlaoise for his portrayal of the Canon in the Little Theatre's production of *Shadow and Substance*.'[14]

During his years as an engineer with the ESB, my father was a foreign affairs commentator on a Radio Éireann programme that also featured Erskine Childers.[15] In the meantime, by mid-1955 (the year my sister EllyMay was born), my father seems to have fallen out of favour at the ESB. I have no information on why this happened. Despite his outstanding academic record, glowing recommendations from extensive previous work experience, and widely acknowledged charm, his superiors turned against him. It is tempting for me, his adoring daughter, to suspect that his stellar record caused jealousy, but the truth is that none of us understands what happened. It is clear from the documentation saved by my mother that, within a year, my father was sending memos to his supervisors informing them that he had completed all assignments, repeatedly pleading for new tasks. Perhaps by doing this he rocked a very tranquil boat. Whatever the reasons, my father's response was to write a play about his experiences at the ESB. My mother was very involved and extremely supportive. I vividly remember the two of them discussing it line by line, laughing and revising the script for hours on end.

When the play, *Man Alive!*, was finished, it was submitted to the Abbey Theatre. The national theatre dithered for some time, but finally decided that the characters would 'soon be identified by rumour', which could open the Abbey to 'the danger of libel actions'. The Abbey requested a rewrite – a revised version that would make it more generic. My parents revised and resubmitted by the autumn of 1958. Ernest Blythe, writing on behalf of the Abbey, replied that the rewriting resulted in a play that would 'henceforth interest only the members of the small class which knows about the frustration which arises in the middle and higher ranges of bureaucracy ...' He added that if the Abbey still had the small experimental theatre it used to have, it would have accepted *Man Alive!* for that venue.[16]

The Gate Theatre then accepted the play, and the very well-respected and established Godfrey Quigley signed on as director.[17] It progressed to full dress rehearsal in the summer of 1960. Some reporters and critics attended the rehearsal and photographs appeared in the press. At that point theatre management summarily cancelled it without explanation. The press took notice of this extraordinary reversal. The drama critic for the *Evening Press* described the play as 'an interesting work ... about Ireland in the here and now. It would be a pity if it remained forever in some bottom drawer.' The theatre columnist of the *Evening Mail* agreed: 'It will be a great shame if this play is not produced.'

At that point the director Jim Fitzgerald, billed as 'the angry young man of Irish Theatre', decided to take matters into his own hands.[18] He approached my parents, saying that he wanted to direct the play and would find a venue. With the uproar still playing out in the press, Leo McCabe of the Olympia Theatre stepped in. He and his partner, Stanley Illsley, offered to run the play for a single week. With Jim Fitzgerald as producer and director, *Man Alive!* premiered on 23 January 1961. In that very large theatre – its capacity was three times that of the Abbey – the play ran to full house audiences every night. Later that year, Illsley and McCabe found another slot, and *Man Alive!* ran for a second week, again with attendance at or close to full capacity. The Olympia produced a billboard and flyers for the premiere that declared 'The controversial comedy about Irish "Big Business" at last gets a showing. The play you had to wait for.' In 1962 *Man Alive!, A play by James D.B. O'Toole* was published by Allen Figgis in Dublin.

Following the production of *Man Alive!*, the ESB assigned my father to the purchasing department. His scientific and engineering talents would never be used there. The production of the play had been his catharsis. He basked in the accolades of the many who were expressing support and admiration for what he had done. I saw the evidence of this when we went for a walk on Dun Laoghaire pier, as we often did on fine evenings, and people came to shake his hand. I saw it, too, when people approached him in St Stephen's Green when mom, as she sometimes did, took us to meet dad when he got out of work. My best-remembered example happened at Tara Street Baths where we attended an annual fundraising event: when my father appeared in his swimming togs to take part in a water polo match, the crowd roared 'Yay Jimmy!' and a group of men standing near me in the observation balcony whistled loudly, their fingers in their mouths.

Not surprisingly, my father set his sights on finding a position somewhere outside of Ireland. At the end of 1963 he discovered that Ohio State University was looking for someone to teach science writing to science, medicine and dentistry students. He was a perfect fit. There was a big catch, however: the position was 'Visiting Professor', meaning that the contract would be for a limited time and the position was not on the tenure track. But the opportunity was so attractive that he took the risk and made the leap. He left for Ohio in January 1964. Between then and Paddy's death in 1967, the two friends saw each other only rarely and fleetingly.

Initially, we stayed in Dublin. My father's time at Ohio State was euphoric. He had great success with the students, and he formed close bonds with other faculty members, particularly with his chairman, George Kienzle, a man my father described as 'lovely'. His university schedule allowed him to spend long holidays with us in Ireland. Kienzle decided to incorporate the programmes my father was developing into the regular curriculum, and he extended my father's contract while he worked to convert the contract from Visiting Professorship to Associate Professorship.

In late 1965, however, Kienzele was diagnosed with cancer and became incapacitated very quickly. As is usually the case in academia, his replacement had the prerogative of making all decisions regarding new programmes and new appointments. His vision did not include placing programmes in science writing ahead of other priorities. My father quickly secured an offer of an Associate Professorship within the Journalism Division of Boston University, and was working there by March 1966. Larry and I joined him there in the autumn of 1966 and my mother, EllyMay and Jaja joined us in 1967.

In Boston my father loved the academic atmosphere and thrived. He established and was the director of a master's programme in science communication. He enjoyed the students immensely, and they selected him as the faculty advisor to their highly regarded student newspaper. My father also applied for and was delighted to be awarded highly competitive grants from the Alfred P. Sloan Foundation, the National Science Foundation and the Herman Cohen Foundation. However, disbursements from grants were then, and still are, controlled by university administrations, and when the then dean used funds from one of the grants to purchase furniture for the faculty lounge, my father was outraged. In his view, the funds should have been spent on student development only and therefore what the dean had done was wrong. He did not have tenure and his position existed at the discretion of the dean, but that did not stop him from objecting vigorously. The dean simply informed him that 'forward-facing presentation', such as the furniture in the faculty lounge, was important for the reputation and image of the university, the recruitment of faculty and students, and that my father's services would no longer be required at the end of his contract.

At the time of his death on 22 February 1973, my father was interviewing for other faculty positions. Based on what he had been told, he was very optimistic that American University in Washington D.C. was preparing an offer for him. Since his departure from Boston University he had been consulting for Arthur D. Little, a management consultancy focused on strategy, technology, and innovation and teaching high school physics and mathematics.

Among the unbearable shafts of grief that devastated me when my father died was one sorrow that struck by surprise. As I mourned my loss of this generous, joyful, playful, child-loving, brilliant, highly ethical man, I also mourned because any children I might have in the future would never know him. Young and unattached as I was at the time, I immediately grasped that the loss would affect not just those of us who loved him, but also those who would come to be loved by us in the future. I now have three children and five grandchildren of my own, and I tell stories about Jimmy O'Toole that help me explain the type of person he was.

One such story took place at Seapoint, our favourite swimming place on the south side of Dublin Bay. Dad would often take us there for swimming, castle-building, shell-collecting, dam-building, and whatever other games we could invent. When he arrived home from work on long summer days, our job was to have our togs and towels packed and be ready to jump into the car for some seaside fun before supper and sunset. Sundays after Mass and breakfast, we would also often head for Seapoint.

One Sunday morning my family and my father's sister, Sheila, and her family were at Seapoint. The tide was almost fully in, with water covering most, but not all, of the swimmers' slips. We had all been swimming, and my father, mother and Aunt Sheila were helping the younger kids dress. A teenage boy ran up to my dad saying: 'Mac, Mac, they need you. They're in trouble.'[19] The boy pointed out at the water where two young women and a man were thrashing around and screaming. My dad immediately dived in and powered his way to them. I could see that one of the swimmers, a young woman, was trying to climb on top of the other two and pushing them under. When my dad reached this panicked woman, he secured her in a cross-chest hold, instructed the other two to hold onto his shoulders, then swam to a large rock which he knew was submerged under the water. He left the two standing on the rock while he proceeded to the shore with the still thrashing young woman. As she was lifted out of the water by some men, my dad kicked off in a hurry to rescue the two other swimmers. What he didn't see was that as the men were pulling the young woman onto the pier, it became apparent that the top of her bathing suit had been lost. Her breasts were bare and very blue from the cold. Upon realizing this, the men panicked and let go of her. She fell off into the deep water and promptly disappeared under the surface.

My mother and Aunt Sheila charged, fully clothed, past the embarrassed men, jumped in, grabbed the young woman and dragged her to safety. Minutes later, my dad, having brought the other two from the rock to the shore, joined us. When he saw my mother soaking wet and shivering, he was baffled. I explained that the men had let the woman fall off the slip because she was topless. My dad replied: 'How could that have happened?' My mom said: 'Never mind how. It just happened. But she'll be all right now.' That was Ireland in the late fifties. Dad took it in his stride.

Another story that reminds me of how large my father's presence could loom occurred in Wexford town in the summer of 1958. My mom had two aunts who were nuns in the enclosed Convent of Perpetual Adoration there. We visited them at least once a year. On this occasion we arrived in Wexford with time to spare before we were expected. It was a gorgeous day, so my parents decided to let us play on the riverbank upstream from the bridge over the Slaney. Dad went with Larry and EllyMay, who was just about to turn three, while I stayed with my mom as she put Jaja into the go-cart. I saw that Larry was sending twigs downstream towards EllyMay and she was glee-fully catching and collecting them.

Suddenly one of the twigs got past her and disappeared under the bridge. Somehow this child decided that she could catch the twig if she ran up the bank, crossed the road, and went down to the other side of the bridge. We all saw her in full stride, ponytail flying, as she ran toward the road filled with fast-moving traffic. Seeing this at the last minute, my father stepped into the traffic, raised both clenched fists over his head, and from somewhere deep within him produced the most astonishingly loud sound: STOP!

The traffic screeched to a halt. I remember a startled cyclist using his feet as well as the brakes. People near me out for a stroll after Mass on this lovely summer Sunday held still. Nothing was moving except the three-year-old child as she continued her dash across the street, determined to retrieve the escaped twig.

My dad was a powerful man, a life-loving man, and I should like my children and their children to know that he could stop traffic in full flow with the force of his presence.

A Child of Clare

ELIZABETH O'TOOLE

I grew up on the Shannon estuary where the river turns to meet the sea and the Atlantic Ocean sweeps in and out of its own volition – where storms were wild and fierce and summer days seemed never-ending. I remember marshes crisscrossed with creeks and dragon flies hovering over pools of mushroom pink, horses standing on three legs, resting in the noonday heat, reeds and bulrushes where waters lapped, and butterflies fluttered over purple thistle tops.

And I remember meadows sweet with summer's scents, wildflowers everywhere, my mother in a print dress, her dark brown curly hair unpinned, bending to pick while humming a sweet air that floats across the clover, mares and foals tossing heads and nosing my mother, for she had been there when the foals were born with soft murmurs of comfort. We were a horsey family, always ready to saddle up and ride.

And I remember running with my brothers and sisters in wild delight to Canny's Hill to swim in the Shannon's best sea water. We were seven, four boys and three girls. We lived in a big house, Ballymorris House on top of Ballymorris Hill. During the Famine, my great-grandfather, Patrick Ryan, had hired the local people to build it. Many were being evicted from their homes and needed work. Those people put something of themselves into Ballymorris House, for it is a warm and friendly house and very beautiful. The people plastered the outside by hand, and when I was growing up you could still see the imprints of their hands. My mother, who knew a lot about art, thought it was the loveliest handiwork she had ever seen.

The house looks out on the Shannon landscape with views across the river to the ruins of Carrigogunnell Castle, a medieval fortification destroyed by the forces of William of Orange in 1691.

In summer I loved to run through our farmland and watch the sun go down in quilts of pink. And in the morning, it would rise and burst through the door of our dairy, brightening the milk buckets and bringing a new day of promise.

A Poet in the House: An Afterword

BRIAN LYNCH

Elizabeth O'Toole's memoir complicates, and in some respects contradicts, the accepted chronology of Patrick Kavanagh's life. Her daughter Margot's response, 'Patrick Kavanagh at Priory Grove', clarifies some of the issues raised by the memoir and it supplies valuable new information, but it also adds to the complications. The passage of time, the fallibility of memory, and the absence of documentation suggest that some of the knottiest of these complications will remain tangled for the foreseeable future. Questions relating to the dates when Kavanagh lived with the O'Toole family occupy much of this Afterword, but in the endeavour to answer them, issues arose that are more substantive and more generally interesting, which may excuse its inordinate length.

Only some of these questions are examined here: the day out at the Punchestown Races, for instance, is not probed other than in notes concentrating on the memoirist's extraordinary memory of the names of toys. Fortunately, the range of dates is quite narrow: Patrick Kavanagh lived with the O'Tooles and their four children at 47 Priory Grove in the Dublin suburb of Stillorgan for an extended period, probably about six months, either from Christmas 1960 to the summer of 1961, or, much more likely, from February 1961 to the summer of that year. According to Antoinette Quinn's biography, however, the poet stayed with the family in 1954.[1] Whenever it happened, it is remarkable that many of the people closest to Kavanagh, including his brother Peter, seem to have known nothing about the episode.

The memoir, though, is not primarily a historical document. It is, instead, a record of domesticity, of daily life with a poet in it, seriously ill when he arrived in the winter but by the summer swimming in the sea at Greystones. This book also includes invaluable photographs of Kavanagh with the family. He is unsmiling, dour, even fierce, wearing the public face he invariably composed for the camera, which is belied by the fact that the O'Toole children patently regard him not as ferocious but as a friend and companion. And his regard for them is clear: he was constantly asking their mother to 'send them down to me. I'm lonely, so very lonely.'

Jim O'Toole's death is the explanation for why so little is known about the Stillorgan chapter in Kavanagh's life: he went to teach at Ohio State University in 1964 and in 1973, at the age of fifty-eight, he died suddenly in Brookline, Massachusetts. Bringing up four children on her own, briefly in Ireland and then in America, while teaching for a living, explains the complete absence of Elizabeth O'Toole from the record. Some of what she heard over the years she thought unjust and, although the memoir is not polemical or contentious, it is underpinned by the desire to correct the injustice. To her, Kavanagh's character was complex and wilful, but also meeker, more vulnerable, less acerbic, warmer than the generally accepted evidence makes him out to be. As a poet, he had a profound influence on Elizabeth and her family, which she wishes to pass on to her children's children. She also wants them to understand and appreciate what an extraordinary man her husband was.

On the face of it this should be a private matter for the family, of interest to the general reader only in so far as it sheds light on Kavanagh. But Jim O'Toole shines out brightly on his own. It is the details that stick in the mind: the image of him, for example, swimming from the Forty Foot in Sandycove to Dun Laoghaire pier and back again, as he did all year round, while reciting to himself Gerard Manley Hopkins' great long poem, 'The Wreck of the Deutschland'.

However, one subject in particular requires scrutiny in this Afterword and by future cultural historians: the rejection of O'Toole's play *Man Alive!* by the Abbey Theatre; its abrupt withdrawal from the Gate Theatre, during dress rehearsal; and its eventual production in the Olympia Theatre. Kavanagh was at the first night in 1961 (as were two future Presidents of Ireland, Erskine Childers and Patrick Hillery) and when the curtain came down to 'thunderous applause', he 'stood up in one of the front rows, turned to face the audience and said, "Remember this applause when you read the reviews in the morning. Newspapers are lily-livered".'[2]

Despite its success with audiences, two separate runs at the Olympia, and publication of the play in book form, *Man Alive!* was to have disastrous consequences for the playwright.[3] This was because the rejection by the Abbey and the Gate had less to do with aesthetics than with the law: both theatres feared being sued for libel. For the newspapers even to report the theme of *Man Alive!* was risky, as can be gathered from the Olympia's programme note:

> Opening in the office of a Large Corporation, a young engineer, an idealist, wants to do his job. He is kicked down by older hands in superior jobs; kicks back against them; gets a bad report; fights against it and doesn't really achieve very much except the retention of his own integrity in the end.[4]

The 'Large Corporation', named in the play the 'Science Production Board', was all too readily identifiable in 1961: Jim O'Toole worked as an engineer in the Electricity Supply Board. It is not known if the ESB threatened to claim that it had been libelled as a body corporate, or if 'older hands in superior jobs' felt they had been defamed personally – there is no mention of any such problem in his ESB personal file.[5] In the event the position of the 'idealist' in the state-sponsored company became untenable and Jim O'Toole, integrity intact, left Ireland for good in 1964. Actually, Jim O'Toole was something of a foreigner in his native land: he was born, brought up and educated in Shanghai, where his father, John, was Assistant Commissioner of Police, and his mother, Ellen (née Bermingham), taught at the Collège Municipal Français and was principal of the Jewish School.[6] It is the facts of John O'Toole's career in China, which in itself is of considerable interest to social historians, that are chosen here as an example of the reliability of the memoir.

One of the most remarkable things about Elizabeth O'Toole is the sharpness of her memory. I began to appreciate how sharp it was only while footnoting relatively minor details. A passing reference, for example, to the painters Mabel Young and Paul Henry, overheard from conversation between Kavanagh and her husband in the front seat of a car while she was in the back, proved to be extraordinarily accurate, down to the description of a stand of beech trees near Mabel Young's house. As a general rule, when Elizabeth misunderstands or mishears something, the mistake turns out to have a basis in fact: she quotes Kavanagh saying that Paul Henry was going to marry Mabel, whereas the marriage had taken place in 1954. It may be the case in this instance that Elizabeth overheard the conversation in that year – she and her husband already knew Kavanagh then.

Elizabeth Ryan was born in 1924 and was brought up in Cratloe, County Clare; her father was a thoroughbred horse breeder and Justice of the Peace, and her mother, née Watson, was a businesswoman and an accomplished amateur pianist from Charleville, County Cork.[7] Elizabeth was educated at Laurel Hill in Limerick, an Irish-speaking secondary school, and at Cathal Brugha Street College in Dublin, graduating with degrees in Nutritional Science and Home Economics Education, followed by a year of training in institutional administration and management.[8] Before her marriage, in

1948, she taught at Drishane Convent in Cork, and as a lecturer at the Church of Ireland College of Education in Dublin, a post to which she was appointed by George Otto Simms, the future Archbishop. She then went on to lecture at Dundrum and Ballsbridge technical schools, and at her alma mater, Cathal Brugha Street College.

By the time Kavanagh came to live in Stillorgan, Elizabeth had four children and no time for teaching. It was quite late in editing the memoir that I inquired about the children's names and ages and discovered that the eldest, Larry, was born in December 1950 and christened Laurence Paul Claudel.[9] It is safe to say that in that year no other child in Ireland was named after the French poet, playwright and diplomat Paul Claudel. The possibility that the O'Tooles, who were committed Christians, shared Claudel's supposed Nazi sympathies and anti-semitism is discussed below, and dismissed.

When it comes to how and why Jim O'Toole's father, John O'Toole, emigrated from Clare to China, it should be borne in mind that Elizabeth is recalling what she heard from her father-in-law, an old man whom she very rarely met. This is what he told her:

> I was sixteen. We were politically unacceptable to the authorities. My father worried I might be arrested and sent in chains to the West Indies, or Australia, so I was rowed out from Galway bay at night to a trawler going to France. I was on my way to Paris where I was supposed to go to college.

Saying 'supposed to' suggests that he didn't go to France – but he did. This raises an important editorial point: at the start of the process, I was inclined to turn some of the many verbatim conversations into indirect speech. Elizabeth O'Toole resisted that approach, and now I think, rightly so. She has a memory for voices and, besides, the memoir is, decidedly, in her own voice.

While John O'Toole was living in Paris, he signed up for the Foreign Legion, but instead of serving in Algeria he chose the French International Police and travelled to Shanghai on the Trans-Siberian Railway (an epic journey, too fleetingly described in the memoir). That the Irish part of the story is questionable is revealed by the entry on John O'Toole in the online archive of the Shanghai Municipal Police. It says he was born in 1878, joined the force in 1900 and – most surprisingly – had previously been a member of the Royal Irish Constabulary.[10]

Elizabeth O'Toole's recollection of what she was told by her father-in-law is probably correct, but some of the detail is undoubtedly wrong. While it is quite possible, for instance, that a young RIC constable could have been suspected by the 'authorities' of having Fenian sympathies at the turn of the century, the time had long passed when such felons, let alone suspects, were transported to Australia – the last convict ship arrived there in 1868.[11] Since John O'Toole's father, a mill-owner in Clare, seems to have had sympathies with the Fenian rebellion of 1867, the reference to convict ships and being sent in chains to the West Indies should probably be heard as the ironic exaggeration of a son remembering a father who feared that history would repeat itself.[12]

One should also consider the possibility that what John O'Toole told his daughter-in-law and the Shanghai police were diametrically opposed; that in Ireland he wanted to cover up his RIC record, and that in China he invented it to enter the police under false pretences. The latter might seem likely were it not for the near certainty that it is false: when John O'Toole arrived in Shanghai, the Chief Superintendent of the force was an RIC officer on secondment, Pierre B. Pattison. Tricking Pattison, without producing papers as evidence of membership, would not have been easy, particularly because by 1900 the links between the RIC and the Shanghai police force were already extensive and long-established.[13] Nonetheless, it is a surprise to discover that the connections between County Clare and Shanghai were deep-rooted in the nineteenth century, and that even in the twenty-first century two Scanlon families in the county 'are known as the Shangs and the Westbys to distinguish them.'[14] Across the Shannon in Kerry there are similar families, such as the Keanes of Listowel, two of whom served in the RIC and in the Shanghai police, while another brother, the playwright John B. Keane, stayed at home. (It is notable that the Abbey Theatre rejected James O'Toole's *Man Alive!* in 1958 at the same time as it rejected John B. Keane's *Sive*, now accepted to be a classic of the Irish theatre.)

The connections to Shanghai were strong on both sides of the O'Toole family. Jim's mother, Ellen, a magisterial figure vividly described in the memoir, was the daughter of Thomas Bermingham, the victim of a famous eviction from the Vandeleur estate in Clare in 1888.[15] His eldest daughter,

Catherine, had three children, a son and two daughters, all of whom were connected to the Shanghai police.

While this Afterword was being written, in January 2020, heated controversy arose over government proposals to commemorate the role of the RIC a hundred years earlier. The most extreme opposition took it for granted that what had been said in 1920 by Eoin MacNeill, a leading republican, was true: 'the police force in Ireland are a force of spies; the police in Ireland are a force of traitors; and the police in Ireland are a force of perjurers'. But in 1902 the *United Irishman*, the Sinn Féin newspaper edited by Arthur Griffith, said:

> The Royal Irish Constabulary is a body of Irishmen recruited from the Irish people; bone of their bone and flesh of their flesh. The typical young constabulary man is Irish of the Irish; Catholic, and (as the word goes) Nationalist; the son of decent parents; his father a Home Rule farmer ... his uncle a patriotic priest; his sweetheart the daughter of a local Nationalist district councillor and patriotic publican. He is smiled on by the Irish clergy; he is smiled on by the Irish girls; he is respected by the young fellows of the street corner and the country crossroads.[16]

In short, when John O'Toole joined the Shanghai police in 1900, he did so as a former member of an Irish police force in good standing with the community. But the situation soon changed drastically: the first victim of the 1916 rebellion was an RIC constable, and during the War of Independence more than 500 RIC men would pay for Eoin MacNeill's definition of them with their lives.

John O'Toole was certainly associated with the Land League – his son's middle name was Davitt – and in Shanghai, according to his granddaughter, he offended his superiors by publicly aligning himself with an unnamed anti-British visitor to the city. By contrast, it appears that Jim was so far from being a sympathizer with violent republicanism that the IRA may have wanted to target him as an informer during the Second World War.

Before examining that subject, two points are worth noting about the tumultuous history of the International Settlements in Shanghai. The first, not mentioned in the memoir, is that in July 1921, when Jim O'Toole was six, the Chinese Communist Party was founded in a house in the French sector near where his mother taught. The second, referred to in passing in the memoir, is that Jim was inter-ested in Pierre Teilhard de Chardin and had heard him lecture. This may have happened in China, where de Chardin lived for many years, though it seems impossible that at the age of eight Jim could have attended lectures the Jesuit philosopher and geologist gave in Shanghai in 1923.[17]

Jim was studying at the Jesuit university in Shanghai when the violence preceding the Sino-Japanese War forced his family to leave the city in 1934. But by 1938 he had degrees from University College Dublin in Mechanical and Electrical Engineering and (like de Chardin) in Geology. Shortly after graduating, the 23-year-old O'Toole went to Germany, arriv-ing in Berlin on 26 February 1939, to work for the giant firm of Siemens-Schukert. The Siemens connection to Ireland was strong: the company had built the Ardnacrusha power plant on the Shannon in the 1920s. By May 1939 Jim was engaged in designing a similar plant to be built in Czechoslovakia. But in September Germany invaded Poland.

Literary historians will immediately wonder if O'Toole knew the novelist Francis Stuart, who would soon be writing scripts and broadcasting for the Nazis. Elizabeth O'Toole does not mention Stuart, nor does she say anything about her husband's experiences in Germany. In fact, what we know is told in 'Patrick Kavanagh at Priory Grove', written by her daughter Margot.

Margot reports that attempts were made in Berlin to recruit her father as part of the alliance between the Chief of Staff of the IRA, Seán Russell, and the Nazis – as an engineer who spoke German (and French, Italian and Mandarin), Jim O'Toole would certainly have been a valuable asset to the IRA and the Abwehr, the Reich's intelligence service. The identity of the recruiter is discussed below, but we know it could not have been Seán Russell: he arrived in Germany from the United States in the first week of May 1940. In any event, Jim O'Toole refused to collaborate with the Nazis. This had serious consequences. According to Margot: 'If he did not immediately understand that the Nazis never took "no" for an answer, a person he described to us only as "a decent German chap" warned him that he was in danger and should flee immediately. He was not able to leave, however, because he had lost his Irish passport. He went into hiding for the next four months.' Since the Irish Legation in Berlin issued her father with a new passport at the end of September 1939, it seems likely that he went into hiding after that date.[18] But to return to Ireland he needed to get a visa that would allow him to enter Belgium. Two days after he got it, at the end of December, he travelled more than 800 kilometres to Ostend and crossed the Channel to Folkestone on 3 January 1940. After some days in London, he travelled by train to Holyhead, took the mail boat and arrived in Dublin on 7 January.

According to Margot, her father was always reticent about the identity of the person who helped him escape from Berlin, but he was not reticent when it came to the security of the Irish state. On the evidence of a close friend, Dr Michael Hayes, now a distinguished emeritus professor of science at Limerick University, as soon as O'Toole returned to Ireland he 'shared with the Irish Government what he had gleaned from the efforts of the Germans to recruit him, an action that … may have exposed him to hostility from the IRA.'[19] This possibility is strengthened by Margot's recollection of attending with her father a private dinner in London for UCD graduates in 1964; also present was 'a small group of English people who spent the evening in high spirits toasting James Davitt Bermingham O'Toole for the important role he had played in England's "most dark and dangerous days".'

Those days had also been dangerous for Ireland. At the beginning of the Emergency, a cohort of German spies, some of them ludicrously inept, landed in the country, intending to disrupt, with the help of the IRA, the government's policy of neutrality.[20] To this end, a German submarine carrying Seán Russell sailed to Ireland in the summer of 1940, but Russell became ill off the coast of Galway, died on board and was buried at sea.[21] Margot comments: 'The mission was aborted.

How much my father knew of all of this is not known, but after he had communicated with the Irish government a Garda Síochána detail kept watch on his parents' home, where he was staying, until the end of the war.'

The relevance of this episode to Patrick Kavanagh, while it is not obvious, is not tenuous. As we have seen, he was in the audience at the first night of *Man Alive!* in 1961 and knew enough about the threat of a libel action to accuse the newspapers of being 'lily-livered'. It seems likely, therefore, that Jim O'Toole had told him the names of his antagonists in the ESB. Kavanagh may have had a conflict of interest here: he was a friend of Patrick Moriarty, who was then the ESB's head of Research and Audit and who would become chief executive in the 1980s, transforming the company into 'a world-class electricity provider'.[22] A much more likely antagonist, though, was James (or Seamus) O'Donovan (1896–1979).

As manager of the Dublin office, O'Donovan was certainly one of the 'older hands in superior jobs' described in the Olympia programme. Kavanagh certainly knew him: he had written for *Ireland To-day*, a magazine founded and edited by O'Donovan between 1936 and 1938. It is very likely that Kavanagh also knew that during the War of Independence O'Donovan had been a member of the IRA headquarters staff, along with Michael Collins; and that he had been interned by the Free State authorities after the Civil War in 1923.

Kavanagh would have learned some of this history from Katherine Moloney, his future wife.[23] Their relationship, which began in 1957 when she was twenty-nine, was intermittent, largely because she lived in London. Nonetheless, by 1961 Kavanagh was probably aware that Katherine's aunt, Mary Christina, known as 'Monty', was O'Donovan's wife. There was an IRA continuity in the marriage: Monty was the sister of Kevin Barry, who was hanged in 1920 at the age of eighteen.[24] And there was another continuity in that Kathy, the eldest of the Barry sisters, was working in the ESB in 1930 and apparently helped O'Donovan get his job in the company.[25]

Kavanagh may also have been told by his friend John Betjeman, who was a British diplomat during the Emergency, that O'Donovan had been 'an asset in place' for the Nazis, though Betjeman could hardly have known then that O'Donovan had the official Abwehr title of 'Agent V-held'.[26] O'Donovan visited Germany three times in 1938; he was involved in sending the novelist Francis Stuart to Berlin with a message that the IRA's radio had been seized by the Gardaí on 31 December 1939; and O'Donovan had himself gone to Hamburg and concluded a deal with the Abwehr in February 1940 to supply arms to the IRA, a plot which foundered when Seán Russell was buried at sea the following August.

If Kavanagh knew anything about the German connection, he did not refer to it in the 16-line verse 'Seamus O'Donavan' [sic], which is a section of a long poem called 'The Christmas Mummers', published in the winter 1954 edition of Nimbus, the magazine edited by the poet David Wright. It is reproduced here with the original punctuation:

> Here comes I Seamus O'Donavan – against the British menace
> I fought when I was younger in the War of Independence;

Encouraged the national language, too old myself to
    learn it —
And if I got a pension who says I didn't earn it?
In days when 'The Emergency' was no poor cow in
    labour
But war most awful threatening the world and our
    neighbour
I took my musket down and joined young men who
    were no moochers
But soldiering nobly for the land into congenial futures;
My face as you can see is clear-marked old IRA,
An Irish face good-natured, Catholic, liberal and gay
My hair is turning whitish (though in youth severely
    mauled,
Oddly, no man who ever fought for Ireland goes quite
    bald).
For the good name of my country I am most insanely
    zealous
And of comrades who got richer I am not the least bit
    jealous
And if you don't believe me and give in to what I say
I'll call in a Successful Statesman and he'll soon clear
    the way.[27]

The reference to O'Donovan being 'severely mauled' prob-
ably refers to the fact that he had blown off three of his fingers
and a portion of his hand in an explosion during the Civil War
in 1922. O'Donovan had a degree in chemistry and went on
to become a self-taught expert in explosives. He was also
the architect of the 'S-Plan', the IRA's bombing campaign

in Britain in 1939 and 1940, which killed ten people and injured many more. Kavanagh knew one of the bombers: the playwright Brendan Behan. Elizabeth O'Toole records Behan being in the audience at the first night of *Man Alive!* but, understandably, she does not mention that when Kavanagh sued *The Leader* magazine for publishing a libellous profile of him, in 1954, he believed Behan was in part responsible for the libel. Three years later Kavanagh was still sore about it: in 1957 he said he was going to emigrate to the moon 'so I wouldn't have to see Brendan Behan any more. It's my only chance to die happy.'[28] In the memoir, Elizabeth O'Toole recalls consoling Kavanagh on the steps of the Four Courts at the conclusion of the libel action.

During the trial Kavanagh had been closely questioned about his vehement denials of friendship with Behan. That three-day cross-examination was conducted by John A. Costello, who subsequently became Taoiseach and was instrumental in getting Kavanagh a sinecure in UCD, in return for a small number of annual lectures. In the memoir Elizabeth O'Toole records what the poet thought of his university patrons: 'They didn't want it said that I died without recognition and with not a penny to my name ... They wanted me buried as Dr Patrick Kavanagh, Professor of Poetry. But God pulled a fast one on them, and I didn't die.' He also thought that 'Your Jimmy' was better qualified to give the UCD lectures because 'his mind is quick. My mind is busy at something else; I have no gift for answers.'

It is curious that Kavanagh suspected the Catholic Archbishop of Dublin, Dr John Charles McQuaid, of having had something to do with the lectureship. According to the memoir, while the poet was in hospital for the operation that removed his cancerous lung in 1954, 'the Archbishop arrived with his entourage and paraded down to Paddy's bed. Paddy said he could only think he was about to die and the Archbishop had come to hear his last confession.' But the poet had difficulty recalling their conversation: 'Had McQuaid said something about giving him a small grant? In any event, soon afterwards Paddy had a visit from some big shots from the university. He thought they had hinted at an honorary doctorate.' According to the memoir, Kavanagh asked if he had to stay alive to receive it, or could it be conferred posthumously. To that query they replied dip-lomatically that 'they were not yet in a position to make any promises ... .'

The fact that the cancer operation was done in 1954 and that the lecture series began two years later is intriguing: none of the biographies links McQuaid to Kavanagh's UCD appointment, though Antoinette Quinn does record that the Archbishop and the College President, Michael Tierney, sepa-rately visited the poet after the operation.[29]

Kavanagh, like all good raconteurs, was prone to exaggera-tion. Of all the events of a life that was largely solitary, desk-bound and sedate, the tale he told of the attempt to murder him in 1959 was the most elaborately decorated.[30] The version Elizabeth O'Toole heard, however, is fantastical in the extreme – and yet again, in the midst of the fantasy, the reader learns new and surprising facts.

According to the memoir, as the poet was making his way home on the frosty night of 19 October 1959, he was attacked, rolled up in a quilt, and tossed over Baggot Street Bridge into the canal (the sodden quilt was found the next day). In the icy water he decided he couldn't blame the perpetrators, 'said a prayer for whoever they were ... stretched out so that he was floating on his back and contemplated the stars.' Eventually he managed to climb out of the canal, crawl across the street and up the steps of a house. After kicking the door, he heard a voice asking who was there by way of a quotation from a poem in Irish, to which the poet managed to reply: '*Tá mé báite, fuar, fliuch*' (I'm drowned, cold, wet). Actually, the poem is the well-known late seventeenth-century ballad *Éamon an Chnoic* which begins:

> *Cé hé sin amuigh*
> *A bhfuil faobhar ar a ghuth*
> *Ag réabadh mo dhorais dúnta?*
>
> *Mise Éamon an Chnoic*
> *Ta báite fuar fluich*
> *Ó shíorshúil sléibhte 's gleannta.*

(Literal translation: 'Who is that outside with the sharp voice ravaging my closed door? I am Éamon of the Mountain, who is drowned, cold, wet from forever walking mountains and valleys.')

Kavanagh's knowledge of Irish was not great, but it is likely that in Kednaminsha National School, which he attended, as in many schools around the country, the children learned

Éamon an Chnoic off by heart. It is, though, hard to imagine that Kavanagh stitched the quotation into the story because he knew that Éamon's surname was O'Ryan and Elizabeth's maiden name was Ryan. But why else would he quote the song? It is, again, impossible to imagine that the memoirist is making it up: what purpose could she have?

Who the Irish scholar behind the door was we are not told, but it certainly was not the woman who eventually opened it. According to Elizabeth, who never names her in the memoir, 'Paddy told me he thought the lady had an Australian accent.' Actually, it was the writer and medical doctor Patricia Avis (1928–77), who was from a wealthy family in South Africa. According to Antoinette Quinn, 'no gossip attached to her relations with Kavanagh. She had her lovers and he was somewhat in awe, even frightened of her, for she had a temper.'[31]

Like Jim O'Toole, Avis is known, if at all, for a single work: her novel *Playing the Harlot*,[32] which includes among its characters her former lovers, the poet Philip Larkin and the then diplomat Dr Conor Cruise O'Brien, as well as her husband, the poet Richard Murphy. Avis, known in Dublin as Patsy Murphy, began writing the novel in 1957 in the Regency house near Roundwood in County Wicklow she had bought from the writers Edna O'Brien and Ernest Gébler. However, in 1958 she went home to her parents in Johannesburg and wrote to Richard Murphy asking for a divorce. The divorce was granted, with custody of their daughter Emily going to him, in 1959.[33] Avis moved back to Dublin that same year and, while finishing the novel, edited and produced four issues of *Nonplus*, a quarterly magazine, which ran until 1960. Kavanagh's contributions to the magazine were, in Antoinette Quinn's words, 'extraordinarily generous', including a number of his best poems.[34] *Nonplus* is relevant not just to Elizabeth O'Toole's memoir but to all other versions of the story, none of which note the fact that the first number was published in October 1959, the month of the canal incident. There is a strong likelihood that when Kavanagh arrived at Wilton Place that night, Patricia Avis already had copies of the magazine in the house.

Alongside work by Flann O'Brien and Donat O'Donnell (Conor Cruise O'Brien), Avis devoted seventeen pages, about a fifth of the magazine, to work by Kavanagh, including three magisterial essays on the subject of violence, nationalism and suffering in literature. Also in the magazine is a review of Tomás de Bhaldraithe's English–Irish Dictionary by an unknown writer, Thomas Hogan, which quotes a number of obscure words in Irish.[35] It seems possible then that Hogan was visiting Avis and that it was him Kavanagh heard on the other side of the door. Obviously, Elizabeth O'Toole could not have invented the voice out of nothing – but then Kavanagh had no apparent reason to invent it either. Why he should refer to it at all is a mystery, but it seems probable that he embroidered the story to please Elizabeth. As for dating *when* he told it, the memoir gives the impression that the canal incident had happened in the distant past. But October 1959 was recent if Kavanagh came to live with the O'Tooles in Stillorgan shortly after Christmas 1960. Actually, the memoir says Christmas but not the year. However, if, as seems likely,

Elizabeth was told the tale in the summer of 1961 or 1962, or even later, an interval of years makes it more credible.

One of the most surprising pieces of new information in the memoir is that immediately after Kavanagh told Elizabeth the story, he rang Patricia Avis and the following week she came to Stillorgan and they went off to spend a weekend together in Wicklow. According to Elizabeth, 'I was harbouring romantic ambitions for Paddy', and when he returned she asked had Avis asked him to marry her, to which he replied, 'No, but she did ask me to go to Australia with her.'

If what Kavanagh said was South Africa, the relationship would not have been all that far from a marriage. But that would presuppose an intimacy that could only have begun almost immediately after her divorce had been finalized in 1959 and she had returned to Dublin from Johannesburg, or perhaps that the relationship had begun even before that, while she was still married to Richard Murphy. The possibility that Kavanagh and Avis were lovers then would complicate our understanding of Murphy's own memoir, *The Kick*.

In that remarkable book, there are very few references to Kavanagh, and all of them are slighting. It is not clear why Murphy should be so antagonistic, but it can hardly have been because the day they first met, in 1950, Kavanagh 'defrauded' him of ten shillings. Their meeting had been initially cordial and, as it happened, significant for Murphy, because Kavanagh introduced him to the diplomat Valentin Iremonger, the poetry editor of *Envoy* magazine, who became Murphy's first publisher in Ireland and a friendly critic. When Murphy said he wanted to buy *The Great Hunger*, Kavanagh said he could get a copy of the Cuala Press edition from the widow of W.B. Yeats, who he was on his way to visit that afternoon; he would, he said, return with it in the evening, but he took the money and didn't come back. The memory rankled: in the five references to Kavanagh in *The Kick* the ten shillings is brought up three times.

The last time Murphy met Kavanagh was in Wilton Place the morning after the canal incident. In the course of giving a statement to a Garda sergeant, Kavanagh denied knowing who had done it, but, Murphy comments disparagingly, 'he knew well who had given him the bum's rush in the dark'.

In Elizabeth O'Toole's version of the story, Patricia Avis bought clothes to replace those Kavanagh was wearing when he was thrown into the canal. Murphy reports the same thing, but in his account, by the time he arrived at his ex-wife's flat that morning, Avis had already gone out and bought Kavanagh a new suit. Murphy then adds: 'At this time she had promised to buy him a bottle of whiskey a day for the rest his life, knowing that he hadn't long to live.' The reader could not be expected to notice that 'At this time' refers not to October 1959 but to October 1967, when he and Kavanagh were both awarded £1,200 by the British Arts Council. According to Avis, when Kavanagh got the news he said to her, 'Too late', which it was: the following month he died. It is unlikely that a writer as meticulous as Murphy could have put his ex-wife's offer of whiskey where it is in the canal bank paragraph by mistake: in 1959 Kavanagh still had eight years left to live. Deliberately or not, the remark reinforces the characterization of the poet as a bottle-a-day alcoholic.

Some of what Murphy says about the relationship is hard to explain. The following example needs some context: he dates it precisely to 3 February 1961, days after *Man Alive!* completed its first run at the Olympia Theatre. The February event, which was held in the ballroom of the Royal Hibernian Hotel in Dawson Street and attended by hundreds of people, was an important occasion for Murphy: it was his first time giving a reading in public. Also on the bill that night were Thomas Kinsella and John Montague, rising stars of Irish poetry. Although he was nervous, Murphy says, 'my training as a choirboy pulled me through, even when Patricia, with an empty glass in her hand, stood up in the middle of [his poem] "Sailing to an Island" and stumbled towards the exit. Through the doorway I could hear from the lobby the loud, rasping cough of Paddy Kavanagh, who had come as far as the ballroom but refused to enter.' In *The Kick* that is the end of the story.

Why Avis should get up drunkenly – as is implied by the empty glass – and stumble out because she heard Kavanagh coughing is not explained. Could it have been simply because she was concerned about his health, or was she too drunk to realize she was embarrassing her ex-husband, or did she do it deliberately, well aware that she was showing less respect for him than she had for Kavanagh? As far as health is concerned, we know from Elizabeth O'Toole's memoir that Kavanagh had been well enough to attend the first night of *Man Alive!* but that when he arrived in Stillorgan he was seriously ill, spitting blood, and soaking wet. The memoir doesn't say what caused the illness or the wetness, merely that Jim O'Toole had found him draped over his car in St Stephen's Green.

It would be fruitless to speculate, just because the Royal Hibernian Hotel (which no longer exists) was about a hundred yards from the Green, that on the night of 3 February, after meeting Patricia Avis in the lobby, Kavanagh, already ill, had wandered around in the sleet and rain (as in the memoir), became even more ill, saw Jim O'Toole's car, and waited for him to turn up. That could have been, in any circumstance, an interminable wait – unless, that is, he knew Jim was also at the reading and, on his way home, could give Kavanagh a lift to his flat in Haddington Road. But that speculation, or any other, is fruitless simply because the memoir does not speculate about it, nor is there any other evidence for it happening.

Nonetheless, *The Kick* does provide, again with great subtlety, a feasible explanation for Murphy's enmity to Kavanagh. At the end of the book, while Murphy was teaching in Tulsa, Oklahoma, in 1994, he records having a dream in which he and Kavanagh climbed 'a penitential cliff' on their hands and knees. A complex and subtle narrative, it is interspersed with painful recollections of Murphy's grievances – the ten-shillings fraud reappears – and of a conversation, dream-like in itself, that he had once had with Kavanagh about quitting Dublin, 'a wretched place', and living in the country (by 1962 Murphy had moved to Cleggan, in the far west of Ireland). Kavanagh said that though he loved the country, 'there are too many ghosts in my village, and I'm afraid of them'.

Murphy then says that Kavanagh 'must have mentioned this conversation to Patricia', because she told him what Kavanagh had said about it: 'It's all right for Murphy to live in Cleggan, because he's a Protestant, so they can't get at him the way they would get at me if I went back to Inishkeen [*sic*].' Murphy then adds immediately: 'On another occasion he had told her, "Murphy has technique, but that's all, and it's not enough".' For a poet who had given his life to poetry, as Murphy had, it was a terrible judgment, and never forgotten. The paragraph that follows is worth quoting in its entirety:

> Now in this morning's dream, as I was waking up, Paddy was in a sublime mood, free of rancour, inspired by the country we had reached at the end of our journey: but he couldn't wait, because he had to get back to Dublin, where he would be meeting Patricia among the dead.

The reader might think that this generous, almost mystical portrait of Kavanagh means that Murphy himself was 'free of rancour'. But he immediately describes getting on the phone from Tulsa to make a long-distance call to Dublin – not an easy thing to do in those days – to tell the novelist Eilís Dillon about the Kavanagh dream of the night before; and when he describes him as 'in a benign mood, free of rancour', Dillon replies, 'That can't be right.' Murphy does say that Dillon was then in hospital, but he doesn't say, though he knew it while writing *The Kick*, that some five months later, on 19 July 1994, she would die there.

However the reader interprets the dream, it supports Elizabeth O'Toole's notion of a romantic relationship between Kavanagh and Avis. Further evidence that he nurtured some kind of ideal passion for her can be found in one of the poems he contributed to *Nonplus* in October 1959. The poem, a sonnet, composed, as he says, a 'short while ago', begins, 'Christmas someone remarked is almost upon us'. Who that someone was he doesn't say, but if he was referring to the Christmas of 1958, it is unlikely that 'us' included Patricia Avis – she seems to have been in London, on her way back to Dublin from Johannesburg. On the other hand, it is possible that she is the 'arrival' in the concluding lines of the poem as they appear in the magazine (which is notably different from the version in the *Collected Poems*):

> Yet there was something about that winter arrival that
>   made me
> Feel younger, less of a failure; it was actually earlier
> Than many people thought. There were possibilities
> For love, for South African adventures, for fathering a
>   baby,
> For taking oneself in hand, catching on without a scare or
> Serving through a world war, joining up at the start of
>   hostilities.[36]

Kavanagh saying that the Christmas of that year 'was actually earlier / Than many people thought' points towards him feeling 'younger, less of a failure' because of something that had happened earlier, perhaps in November. It is not known when Avis arrived back in Dublin, but it is just about possible to think that when she did, Kavanagh immediately fell in love with her.

The phrase in the poem 'catching on without a scare' is curiously unidiomatic: what kind of 'scare', unless it is a misprint for 'care', could Kavanagh and/or Avis have felt? It is also slightly odd that the poet, describing his current situation, should refer to 'a world war': the last World War had ended in 1945, and in 1958 the only possible world war would have been nuclear, which would not have involved 'joining up'.

It is speculation to imagine that when Kavanagh wrote a 'short while ago', he and Avis had been discussing the possibility of going off to live in South Africa because she was pregnant, but that it turned out to be merely 'a scare'. Moreover, it is speculative to suggest that when Kavanagh wrote the poem, at some time in 1959, he was remembering that at Christmastime in 1958 Avis feared Richard Murphy's reaction when her pregnancy revealed itself and he discovered that Kavanagh was the father. But that speculation has to allow for the fact that Avis would have had to have become pregnant some months earlier, which could not have happened because, for most of 1958, she was in Johannesburg.

In *The Kick* Murphy describes at some length how much Avis suffered during her periods: it seems that she endured chronic pain for years and that, as Kavanagh did with his gastric illness, she treated it with alcohol – and with the pills she eventually took to end her life in 1977. Seventeen years later, in 1994, when Murphy dreamed of Patricia 'among the dead', he was old enough, sixty-seven, to feel the end of his own life was near, and even nearer when *The Kick* was published in 2002.

If these facts are relevant and the speculations have any validity, it is possible to think that the 'war' Kavanagh refers to in the sonnet is the one that was about to break out between Avis and her husband. But in that reading the tense makes a difference to its tone. It gives to the poem an air of regret: there had been possibilities a 'short while ago', but they are gone now. On the other hand, it must be the case that when Kavanagh arrived soaking wet on 19 October 1959, Avis knew that he had once thought her homeland might be home to him: it says so in the poem.

Kavanagh and Avis remained close: in Peter Kavanagh's biography of his brother, *Sacred Keeper*,[37] a letter from Patrick gives his address as 1 Wilton Place. Antoinette Quinn also records that he was a 'frequent visitor' to Wilton Place, and that Patricia drove Patrick to Inniskeen as late as March 1965.

Like Jim O'Toole's, Avis's career was blighted by the fear of libel: a director of Faber and Faber in London, Charles Monteith, rejected *Playing the Harlot* 'because it slandered his friends'.[38] That happened in 1963. According to the introduction to the novel, it was 'about this time' that Avis entered into a relationship with T. Desmond Williams (1921–87), Professor of Modern Irish History at UCD. That vagueness allows for the possibility of the relationship having begun in 1962 when Avis asked Kavanagh to go to 'Australia'. As it happens, this editor studied history under Desmond Williams between 1963 and 1966. Because UCD was then in Earlsfort Terrace and Wilton Place is nearby, I saw him often walking between the two places. He was not at all impressive to look at: a pale, sickly, rather flabby little man with a limp (the result of a schoolboy injury).[39] Intellectually, however, Williams was a giant, but of a peculiarly passive sort: although he had a large brain, what came out of it was puny, relatively speaking. Ill-health probably played a part in his small output: he chain-smoked cigarettes throughout his dazzling lectures, delivered in a slightly stammering monotone, on Machiavelli and the Balance of Power in Europe. At the time I was vaguely aware that he had had some kind of special access to British diplomatic papers – but not that he had been given a nominal military rank in the British security forces to allow him to go to Berlin in the 1940s to study papers on foreign policy captured by the Allies. This privileged experience should have led to Williams becoming in public what he was in private: a leading authority on Hitler and Nazi Germany. Why that did not happen is not known.

In 1954, the year Patrick Kavanagh sued *The Leader* magazine for libelling him in an anonymous 'Profile', Desmond Williams was also sued for libel, following publication by *The Leader* of an article in which he alleged that the former Ambassador to Spain, Leopold Kerney, had had Nazi sympathies.[40] According to Antoinette Quinn, a 'reliable source' told her that it was Williams who had written the profile of Kavanagh in *The Leader*, and there is certainly evidence that he was closely connected to the poet and diplomat Valentin Iremonger, now widely accepted to be its author.[41] Kavanagh, of course, lost – but Kerney won. Before the case could go to the jury, it was settled, with damages, and with a full apology from Williams.

The libel action related to a meeting in 1942 between Ambassador Kerney and a Nazi leader, Edmund Veesenmayer, who would be responsible for transporting hundreds of thousands of Hungarian Jews to the death camps in 1944; at his Nuremberg trial he got a twenty-year sentence, but served only ten. However, at the beginning of 1939, when Jim O'Toole arrived in Berlin, Veesenmayer was still something of an apprentice war criminal, making himself rich in the banking business and interfering, to malignant effect, in the internal affairs of Serbia and Croatia. Then, in March 1940, he was tasked, apparently by Hitler himself, with subverting Irish neutrality.

Long before that date, Veesenmayer had contact, direct and indirect, with IRA leaders in Ireland, including the ideologically pro-Nazi James O'Donovan.[42] It seems likely that O'Donovan kept him informed of arrivals to the very small Irish community in Berlin, especially if they were republicans with pro-German leanings. But Jim O'Toole does not fit that bill. Unlike the Michael Davitt from whom he got his middle name, he seems never to have espoused political violence, nor any kind of anti-semitism – not surprising in someone whose mother had been principal of a Jewish school in Shanghai; nor does he appear to have been engaged in party politics at any time in his life.[43] Like Michael Davitt, he was left-leaning, a social liberal; and, while sceptical of the influence of the clergy, he and his wife were progressive Catholics, very interested, for instance, in the writings of Teilhard de Chardin.

Nonetheless, it is necessary to test the hypothesis that when O'Toole was a fiery young man, he had been a Nazi sympathizer. This appears to be borne out by a document in which an unnamed MI5 officer in Britain noted in January 1940, according to the historian Eunan O'Halpin, that it was 'galling to have to grant passage to people such as an Irish employee of Siemens who was plainly going to make a contribution to the German war effort'.[44] It is more than likely that the MI5 officer was referring to Jim O'Toole, but if designing a hydro-electric plant for Czechoslovakia – work that began before the war started – was 'plainly' intended to help the war effort, his commitment to the Nazi cause was short-lived, and as soon as he could he returned to Ireland. The malign interpretation – that O'Toole had been sent to Berlin by the IRA on some secret mission and was then sent back to Ireland by Veesenmayer or someone unknown in the Abwehr – seems too remote to be given credence. One would have to believe, for instance, that the IRA had not one but two agents operating on secret missions in Berlin at more or less the same time: the first being James O'Toole, who arrived back in Dublin, via London, on 7 January 1940, and the second being Francis Stuart, who set out from Dublin to go to Berlin shortly after 31 December 1939, the day the government had seized the radio the IRA used to communicate with the Abwehr. Jim O'Toole could not have known that.

In addition, historians have by now identified even minor Irish collaborators with Nazi Germany, and James O'Toole's name does not figure amongst them, nor is there any record of him playing any part in IRA activities during the Emergency.[45] Had his mission been significant, and had he been at all prominent in the IRA, he would certainly have come to the attention of G2, the highly efficient intelligence service, and been interned in the Curragh military camp along with many others, including, in 1942, James O'Donovan. Less mercy would have been shown to Jim O'Toole had he used a gun: the de Valera government shot or hanged a number of IRA men who had attacked the security forces of the Free State.

As for Kavanagh's own politics, little can be said here, except to refer in passing to a book he had probably read 'hundreds of times': Frederick Rolfe's *Hadrian the Seventh*, a brilliant fantasy about an English Pope who is a believer in papal absolutism and an enemy of socialism.[46] Kavanagh was a non-dogmatic supporter of Fine Gael, the conservative party supported by the strong farmer class (although he did not belong to that class), and he was certainly religious. On the other hand, many of the people he mixed with were irreligious, anti-clerical, socialistic, semi-retired IRA men, the exact opposite of himself. It is also remarkable, at a time when homosexual acts were criminal, how many of Kavanagh's closest friends were gay, including, allegedly, Archbishop McQuaid. The notion that there might have been a homosexual element in the relationship between them is not as absurd as it seems: when they first got to know each other, the young poet and the priest were close enough for Kavanagh to sign off a letter with the word 'Love'. The more recent view, that he regarded the Archbishop as too mighty for his own good, is supported by Elizabeth O'Toole's memoir, though it is notable that, unlike Antoinette Quinn, she does not say that Kavanagh cynically exploited McQuaid as a source of money.

Kavanagh's friends were very various and, especially in the pubs of Dublin and London, they were often drunken. This was not at all unusual then: many workers and not a few employers drank during working hours. But alcohol and pubs do not figure at all in Elizabeth O'Toole's memoir. As the mother of four children, she had neither the time, the patience, nor the inclination for drinking. Nor, when he was living in Priory Grove, had Kavanagh. This goes counter to the image painted by those who saw him as he 'threw/ Back large whiskeys in the corner of a smoky bar'. Margot, it is true, does say that in the mornings, while he was at the typewriter, Kavanagh always had a naggin of whiskey in his pocket, but, as he says in the same poem:

> ... if only I would get drunk it wouldn't be so bad;
> With a pain in my stomach I wasn't even comic,
> Swallowing every digestive pill to be had.[47]

In the face of all the evidence, and Kavanagh's own frequent confessions, it would be futile to deny his often extreme drunkenness at this time – and yet in the memoir he is always sober.

Elizabeth O'Toole's memory is most reliable when she describes events at which she was present. Her first-hand evidence, however, can be complicated by the omission of information that she knew at the time but has now forgotten. A good example is her story of how and why Kavanagh wore a dinner jacket owned by 'the Gorgeous Gael' Jack Doyle (1913–78) at what she describes merely as a first night in the theatre.[48]

Like almost everyone in Ireland in the 1940s, Kavanagh was fascinated by Doyle's rags-to-riches rise to fame as a heavyweight boxer, a Hollywood film star, and a popular singer. He even wrote a verse entitled 'Jack Doyle', which, though brief, explains something of the reasons for both his own and the general fascination:

Some think he might have won the crown

That now to Brown Joe's head seems glued,

But he got tangled in the gown

Of Venus waiting, as she would,

For the handsome boy who comes to town.[49]

The reference to 'Brown Joe' is to Joe Louis, known as the Brown Bomber, who was World Heavyweight Champion from 1937 to 1949. The notion that Doyle's downfall was due to an entanglement with Venus now seems absurdly sexist, but it was commonly believed then. The verse was probably written not long after Doyle returned to Ireland from Hollywood with his wife, the Mexican film star Movita, in 1943. The stage show they put on in the Theatre Royal, then one of the biggest theatres in Europe, was hugely popular, but its witty title, 'Punch and Beauty', was all too accurate. When drunk, which was often, Doyle could be psychotically violent, especially to Movita, who, in search of a quiet life, went back to Hollywood and married Marlon Brando. When sober, Jack Doyle was charming, gentle and extravagantly generous – which explains the gift of his jacket to Jim O'Toole. In 1943 it was of little use to Doyle: by then he had ballooned to over 18 stone in weight.[50] Nonetheless, the fact that, with some adjustments, Kavanagh was able to wear it in 1961 is an indication of how burly a man the poet was.

According to Elizabeth O'Toole, Kavanagh and her husband – but, significantly, not herself – attended the first night and had 'a whale of a time. It turned out to be a big affair. Patrick Kavanagh was the guest of honour, and the evening was a tremendous success.' This is echoed by

Antoinette Quinn, who says Kavanagh 'showed up on the opening night in evening dress' – Jack Doyle's tuxedo – and that the occasion was the premier of *Gamble No Gamble* in the Abbey Theatre on 1 June 1961, which, Quinn says, 'met with a rapturous reception'.

Elizabeth O'Toole is both right and wrong to say that Kavanagh was 'the guest of honour'. In fact, it was the first night of a ballet and he was the author of the poem on which it was based. Commissioned by Patricia Ryan, Director of the Irish National Ballet, the poem was spoken by T.P. McKenna (1929–2011), one of the finest actors of the era; and the music, played by a forty-piece orchestra, was composed by Archie Potter (1918–80), a pupil of Ralph Vaughan Williams, and Professor of Composition at the Royal Irish Academy of Music. The choreographer, Patricia Ryan (?–2011), was the wife of John Ryan, editor of *Envoy* magazine, but she would soon marry the painter Patrick Collins (1911–1994), the winner of the Guggenheim Award in New York in 1958.

By any standard, *Gamble No Gamble* was a significant social and cultural event at a time when theatre, if not ballet, was popular across all classes. Kavanagh was well aware of this, so when he was invited to the premiere by Patricia Ryan and asked her, in Quinn's words, 'What would I be doin' lookin' at a lot of wimmen leppin' around the stage', he was probably being sarcastic about the not uncommon opinion of him then as an ignorant peasant.

According to the Quinn biography, it was only with great difficulty that Patricia Ryan was able to prise scraps of verse out of Kavanagh. However, while much of the libretto is, as

Quinn shows, identical to his poem, 'The Gambler: A Ballet', there is some confusion about which came first.[51] The poem was commissioned by the Guinness company for the Poetry Book Society's Festival of Poetry at the Mermaid Theatre in London, but it appears that Kavanagh plagiarized the poem from the libretto and not the other way round. Unfortunately, most of the theatrical text, apparently one hundred and seventeen lines of verse written in triplets, is now lost. It is often assumed that Kavanagh's manuscripts were disorderly, but in fact he typed and kept carbon copies of almost all his letters, as can be seen in the Kavanagh Archive in UCD. The casual style of his late poetry has led to the assumption that he tossed off verses carelessly, perhaps drunkenly, whereas, from a technical point of view, writing triplets, a variation of Dante's *terza rima*, which is relatively easy in Italian, is infernally difficult to do at any great length in English.

Kavanagh was the Irish judge of the Guinness Poetry Award from 1959 to 1961, the year of the *Gamble No Gamble* ballet, but in the memoir he is described as judge of a competition held by *The Observer* newspaper, almost certainly in 1962. As far as can be learned, there was no such competition, but Elizabeth O'Toole gives a vivid description of the poet despairingly slogging through sacks of entries trying, with the help of her children, to find a decent poem. When he found one, he stopped reading the other entries.

There are two references to Jim O'Toole in Antoinette Quinn's biography. As we shall see, one is problematic. The other is relatively straightforward and it indicates a closeness to Kavanagh not previously understood. According to Quinn, a stage version of *Tarry Flynn* 'had been mooted several times in the 1960s' and John Ryan had 'attempted to get Kavanagh's agreement to a Gate production in February 1962, telling him that the theatre was available in March.' Quinn continues: 'In April of that year Jim O'Toole enquired if Kavanagh would give him permission to turn the novel into an Abbey play ... Nothing came of either Ryan's or O'Toole's initiative.'[52]

In fact, it is remarkable that six days after John Ryan wrote his letter, on 2 February, Jim O'Toole also wrote to Kavanagh. It is not known how the poet responded to Ryan, but the UCD Kavanagh archive contains a series of letters from O'Toole on the subject. The first, dated 8 February, reveals that the poet was no longer living in Stillorgan and how warm their relationship continued to be: Jim says how distressed he had been to see Kavanagh 'ill the other day in hospital', which 'explained only too well why I could not pick you up for our evening together last Monday to which the family had been eagerly looking forward' – the 8th was a Thursday, the 5th a Monday. Referring to the play, he says, 'Already I have the shape of the situations boiling', and he adds, 'A Kavanagh play without the benefit of the Theatre Festival handouts would be the cultural event of this year, or any year, in this country, or any country', and signs off, 'Yours ever Jimmy O'Toole'. Since there is no other reference to the Festival in the letter, it is likely that while he visited Kavanagh in hospital, they had discussed the best time for the play to be put on. As the national theatre, the Abbey, unlike other theatres, did not receive financial support from the Festival, the implication is that *Tarry Flynn* was more prestigious.

From the next letter, dated 16 February, it is clear that Kavanagh has not yet agreed, because Jim O'Toole says, 'If you authorised me to work on the stage version of *Tarry Flynn* it would take a lot of the sting of the next two months off you.' (What Kavanagh was doing during that two-month period is discussed below.) O'Toole goes on to suggest how they would work together: 'Day by day I'd call on you to report progress', adding that the play's 'financial prospects are bright'. The next sentence, interesting in itself, is editorially curious: a portion of the letter has been cut off the page. What remains is this: 'If you use me without any concessions to Beckettism or Behan …' The word is clearly not the complementary 'Behanism'; it looks more like 'Behanesque', but what the phrase reveals is O'Toole's stylistic standard: as in *Man Alive!*, the play would be pitched somewhere between Behan's music hall and Beckett's theatre of the absurd, perhaps closer to the expressionism of Sean O'Casey (whom Kavanagh greatly admired and respected).

By 12 April, the date of the next letter, Kavanagh still hasn't made up his mind. Addressing him as 'My Dear Paddy', O'Toole says he is 'daily hoping to hear from you … How's the form? … Please don't let the project of dramatizing your book go by default.' The following day Kavanagh at last replies (edited here):

> Dear Jim, sorry for the delay. I was intending to write everyday but went lazy. I am only too willing that you should make Tarry Flynn into a play. But wouldn't it be better to ask Blythe would he be interested? 50-50 basis

> of course. But it would have to be collaboration between
> us both … it might be fun, All the best Patrick Kavanagh[53]

The reference to Ernest Blythe, Managing Director of the Abbey, suggests a reason why the dramatization was either not written or rejected: that Jim O'Toole contacted Blythe and was rebuffed. The context was unfavourable: in 1962 the Abbey was in turmoil because the artistic director, Ria Mooney, was being replaced by Tomás Mac Anna, a process completed by her resignation the following year. That Kavanagh was willing to collaborate with O'Toole indicates how much he respected him. That the Abbey thought highly of him, too, is borne out by looking at Blythe's letter rejecting *Man Alive!*. Like almost everything else about this former Minister for Finance and violently republican Northern Protestant, the letter is surprising. Readers, especially if they were not taught Irish at school, will have some difficulty appreciating how devoted Blythe was to the revival of the language. Nothing in the letterhead is in English, and the only indication that 'Amharclann na Mainistreach' is the Abbey has been typed in by a typist, who, as if sceptical, adds a question mark to 'Theatre'. But even a person who went to an Irish-speaking school and who has some knowledge of the history of Irish drama, like this editor, will pause before realizing that one of the Directors, 'Leamhnach Robastún', was the Protestant playwright Lennox Robinson. (It is worth noting that Archbishop McQuaid decreed that any Catholic who attended Robinson's funeral in Saint Patrick's Cathedral would be committing a mortal sin. Only one Abbey actor risked hellfire, but he or she remains anonymous.)

Robinson knew Jim O'Toole well enough to be photographed with his daughter Margot in a group that includes the sculptors Henry Moore and F.E. McWilliam and the architect Michael Scott. The photo was taken in Stephen's Green in 1954. But it is not likely that Robinson read *Man Alive!* – he died in 1958. Ernest Blythe, however, appears to have read two drafts of the play and, as his letter of rejection shows, he was in two minds about both of them. What is doubly surprising is that he preferred the first draft and had been very inclined to put it on, even though it was plainly 'a slashing attack on the ESB' and identifiable individuals were being 'pilloried'. Nonetheless, while Blythe says that 'nobody would have minded its exaggeration and one-sidedness', it is probable that he wanted to give the playwright this impression. As he then makes clear, the Abbey was unable and unwilling to risk a libel suit. But the result of removing any reference to the ESB in the second draft, in Blythe's view, 'took from the immediacy of the exposition' of the central character's 'grievance and anger'.

The judgment is acute: in the version of *Man Alive!* published by Allen Figgis in 1962, the absence of the ESB and recognizable individuals is at once obvious and vague. As a consequence, the plot is nebulous and what the central character, Tim O'Malley, is angry about is unfocused: without the conflict between Jim O'Toole and the ESB over what was then the premier industry in the State – the engineering of the energy supply – the comedy is Kafkaesque but without Kafka. But this is a presumption because, although the O'Toole family has kept an archive of papers, the first draft of the play remains to be identified. Even as it stands, however, *Man Alive!* is a fascinating representation of contemporary thinking about a stagnating society just before entering a period of rapid industrialization. It is also revealing of Jim O'Toole's decidedly Christian philosophy: Tim O'Malley tells a Franciscan priest, Father Aidan, who is in effect his alter ego, that, 'Every job of work [is] a work of art and every work of art a bridge to God, and on every bridge a happy man'. While it could be said that this thought and *Man Alive!* as a whole is a theatrical expression of Patrick Kavanagh's credo, it lacks the poet's particularity. This failing was observed by Patrick O'Connor, the drama critic of the then leading Catholic journal, *The Furrow*. There was, he said, 'a basic unreality, to my mind, about the corporation in the play, a vacuity in the character of the engineer that forestalled my sympathy, and an unconvincing air of contrivance about the dilemma in which he places himself.'[54] This opinion had a personal edge to it: O'Connor had been a close friend of Kavanagh for years, and almost certainly knew Jim O'Toole, but the friendship had cooled by 1956 when the poet, in the second lecture he gave at UCD, apparently made a disparaging remark about O'Connor. This was probably because Kavanagh had been shortlisted to be appointed Curator of the Municipal Art Gallery in Parnell Square, but O'Connor had got the job.[55] By January 1960, however, a scandal over the Curator's role in the Gallery's purchase and sale of paintings by the eighteenth-century Guardi brothers forced O'Connor to resign.

Antoinette Quinn's biography says that Kavanagh stayed with the O'Tooles for an indeterminate period at some time after June 1954, and that he did so at the invitation of 'Jim O'Toole, an engineer and after-hours dramatist'. This latter description is questionable: *Man Alive!* was then still years in the future. The description of O'Toole as 'a firm believer in the poet's genius' who offered Kavanagh 'a warm room, regular meals and the leisure to produce another *Tarry Flynn*' sounds plausible, and seems to be conclusively proved by the information that O'Toole and his unnamed wife had 'two small children at the time'. In the memoir, however, and in Margot O'Toole's account, and in the family photographs, there are four children. The mention of *Tarry Flynn* also suggests the later date, when Jim O'Toole proposed adapting the novel for the stage.

The problem with Quinn's version is that there is, frustratingly, no evidence for it in the biography's endnotes: in fact there are no notes at all for the post-June 1954–1955 period, other than a general statement that the chapter is based on conversations with a number of sources – but amongst them is Dr Sheila Lawlor, Jim O'Toole's sister. It seems certain that Sheila was the source of Quinn's description of her brother, and that it was she who warned Jim about the danger that Kavanagh's 'spitting prolifically indoors in the children's vicinity' could infect them with tuberculosis. To this Jim 'responded that he was aware of the problem but the man was such a genius he felt he had to tolerate it.' Quinn observes tartly: 'Such was the veneration Kavanagh inspired in some quarters.'[56] But, although Elizabeth O'Toole does record her alarm at seeing the poet spit blood the night he arrived at Priory Grove, she does not record it happening thereafter and, as with the drunkenness, it is hard to imagine that if the spitting were prolific she would have venerated Kavanagh above her own flesh and blood.

Since Quinn published her biography in 2001, almost half a century after 1954, and since the source for the information was Dr Lawlor, who can only have been an occasional visitor to her brother, it would be understandable if either she, or Antoinette Quinn, or both of them together in conversation, dated the event to 1954 and forgot that it happened in 1961.[57] The most logical explanation is that Sheila was reporting to Quinn what her brother and sister-in-law had told her about Kavanagh spitting blood when he arrived in Stillorgan, but conflated it with a memory of what she had been told by Jim and Elizabeth about Kavanagh in 1954, a time when the O'Tooles had only two children.

It is also worth noting that Sheila Lawlor's husband was an engineer with the ESB and that Kavanagh had made strenuous attempts to get the permanent and pensionable job, then being advertised, of PR spokesman for the company. Quinn records this from the diary of Padraig O'Halpin, who was also an ESB engineer, a published poet, an admirer of Kavanagh, and father of the historian Eunan O'Halpin.[58] Bearing in mind that the poet was also connected to James O'Donovan and to Patrick Moriarty, its future chief executive, the number of people Kavanagh knew in the ESB is remarkable.

An added difficulty for Quinn in recording Kavanagh's life was his secretiveness: he kept himself to himself. We know from Elizabeth O'Toole's memoir, for instance, that the Artistic Director of the Abbey Theatre, Ria Mooney, had to search to find him in Stillorgan. We know, too, that the first the Kavanagh family knew of his marriage to Katherine Moloney in 1967 was when he rang his sister Annie on the day of the wedding and wept in telling her the news. The O'Toole memoir records him weeping on another occasion: hanging out the washing with Elizabeth reminded him of his mother. It was from that moment on that Kavanagh formed a bond with her, and with her children – he needed their company because, as he said, he was 'so lonely'.

During the editing process it appeared possible that Kavanagh stayed with the O'Tooles not in 1961 but in 1962. Examining the later period, however, illuminates the earlier one in ways that are surprising; it also serves to show that the relationship continued after the poet had left Priory Grove.

According to Antoinette Quinn, Kavanagh was so ill on 28 December 1961 that he was admitted to Baggot Street Hospital with 'acute gastritis, a consequence of the alcoholic poisoning brought on by over-indulgence at Christmas', and with malnutrition, for which he was 'given injections to improve his appetite'. No doctor is cited in the endnotes and, as usual, the chapter is prefaced by a list of sources, but none appears to be relevant to the Baggot Street Hospital illness.

Quinn does not say where Kavanagh spent the Christmas of 1961; she does say, however, that Katherine Moloney was in Dublin and stayed with her family at 4 Winton Road, Rathgar. In any event, the seriously ill and malnourished poet of 28 December made a rapid recovery: by 6 January he was an 'outpatient', convalescing in Inniskeen with his sister Annie. There, Quinn says, 'the presence of a nurse and an orderly domestic routine helped him to feel safe.' Five weeks later, on 14 February, he was back in Baggot Street with pneumonia caught by sleeping in a damp bed 'during a weekend visit to Dublin' – later in the chapter it emerges that the reference is to the room he rented in Upper Mount Street from an old friend, Violet McWeeney.

Quinn reports that while Kavanagh was in Baggot Street Hospital in February he was visited by another old friend, Leo Holohan, a senior civil servant. The reference is to Holohan's article 'A Tribute', published in *The Irish Times* on 1 December 1967, shortly after the poet's death. But in the article Holohan says only that the hospital visit happened 'a few years ago'. It may be that Quinn spoke to Holohan about the matter, but if so, she does not include him in the usual list of sources at the beginning of her endnotes.

Holohan's 'Tribute' is very much in agreement with both Elizabeth and Margot O'Toole's attitude: he disliked the hostility directed at Kavanagh. But interpreting hostile remarks about the poet frequently requires an understanding of tone. This is how Quinn reports, for instance, Kavanagh's convalescence in Inniskeen with Annie: 'Ingrate that he was, he publicly attributed' his recovery to the country air 'rather than to her devoted care'. It was almost certainly Annie who described him as an 'ingrate', which was a sisterly barb, and more or less affectionate. If she meant it, her tone was quite different in the letter she had sent him on 5 March: 'Any sign of you coming up to Mucker? ... I've got the bookshelves up', but she would let him put up the books himself, signing off, 'Cheerio and good health, Annie'.

Kavanagh had become chronically restless after 1958, when he left the large flat at 62 Pembroke Road where he had lived for 15 years. Before leaving he 'walked into each room in turn and prostrated [himself] on the floor' and wept.'[59] From then on, as Quinn notes, he became a nomad, an apt word considering this chronology:

28 December 1961	Kavanagh very ill in Baggot Street Hospital.
6 January 1962	He is well again and goes to Inniskeen.
Sometime before 14 February	He comes back to Upper Mount Street for a weekend, and sleeps in a damp bed.
Circa 21 February	Leo Holohan visits him in hospital.
Circa the same date	The actor T.P. McKenna visits. Invites Kavanagh to stay with him in Sandymount Avenue.
After 11 days	McKenna's wife says he can't stay any longer. The guest room has to be redecorated and the carpet thrown out.
Circa 2 or 3 March	Kavanagh goes back to Inniskeen and stays there for 'most of April and May', but he is drinking hard, taking the bus into Dundalk because he is barred from McNello's pub in Inniskeen.
On 13 April	Kavanagh approves a stage adaptation by Jim O'Toole of *Tarry Flynn*.
Early May	According to Quinn, Katherine Moloney is back in Dublin and she and Kavanagh 'met for a few days'.
'Late Spring 1962'	*Tarry Flynn* is published in paperback.
'Much of summer 1962 ...'	... 'is spent in Inniskeen', Quinn says, correctly, because Kavanagh writes a poem for John Jordan that begins 'I am in a garage in Monaghan. / It is June'.[60]

This chronology does not include what must have been a visit of some days by Larry Sheedy, the editor of the *Irish Farmers Journal*, who, with Kavanagh's 'connivance', posted copies of *Tarry Flynn* to six of the original characters in the book, and then went to Inniskeen to interview them.[61]

A cheap edition of *Tarry Flynn* (it cost two shillings and sixpence, about 12 cent in euro) was published by Four Square, an imprint of the New English Library, in 'late Spring' 1962, according to Quinn, but a royalty statement in the UCD archive indicates that it came out in January ('1.1962') and by the end of the year had sold an astonishing 13,303 copies, earning Kavanagh royalties of £126, somewhat short of his advance of £150. (The book is extremely hard to find: as of February 2020 only one was to be found on the Internet, from a seller in County Cavan.)

The sales figures would have been of considerable importance to Jim O'Toole: he and Kavanagh had agreed to collaborate on dramatizing what was becoming a huge best-seller; and after the *Man Alive!* disaster of the previous year O'Toole would at last be recognized by the national theatre. But, while Kavanagh's letter agreeing the deal is in the UCD archive, there is no script by Jim O'Toole, or by John Ryan, and the adaptation that was staged in the Abbey in 1966 was done by P.J. O'Connor.

Of course, if Kavanagh was living in Stillorgan, he cannot have stayed with T.P. McKenna in Sandymount. According to Quinn, after Kavanagh had been in the McKenna house in Sandymount for a week, the actor's wife, Mai, 'could endure it no longer': the maid refused to clean his room and he was 'peeing in the front garden'. When Mai asked him to leave, Kavanagh said, 'I pity you. You're an ignorant woman', and never spoke to her again. Unfortunately, this confrontation is not footnoted and though the probable source for the entire episode seems to be T.P. McKenna, he is listed merely as one of seventeen people with whom Quinn had conversations, probably in the 1990s, thirty years after the event. While there is no shortage of reports of Kavanagh behaving badly, what he said to Mai McKenna is inexplicable but of a piece with him spitting prolifically in the O'Toole household.[62]

The Holohan 'tribute' is noted in Quinn, but Holohan is not mentioned in the list of sources prefacing the endnotes; nor is Annie Kavanagh, but she is quoted in the text, so she is probably the source for her brother being barred in McNello's pub in Inniskeen. Quinn does not say how she knows Katherine Moloney was in Dublin in early May, but the information almost certainly came from Katherine, because Quinn then writes a long paragraph about her moving flats in London and how much Kavanagh liked getting letters from her – he kept, we are told, sixty-five of them, but not where they are held, though if they were the source of the information one would expect a citation. Quinn says Kavanagh and Katherine 'met', which suggests she was staying with her parents, but not where he was staying, presumably in Mount Street, or with Leland Bardwell in Leeson Street – but, unless all the evidence in the biography is wrong, it could not be Stillorgan.

As can be seen in the memoir, Ria Mooney, the Abbey's Artistic Director, came to the O'Toole house in Stillorgan to invite Kavanagh to the premiere of *Gamble No Gamble* and he attended, wearing Jack Doyle's tuxedo, on 1 June 1961. What Elizabeth O'Toole does not mention, perhaps because she did not know it, was that there was considerable tension between Kavanagh and Mooney: in 1947 he had denounced her lover, the poet F.R. Higgins, as 'a phoney, a Protestant in stage-Irish costume', despite the fact that Higgins had been very kind to him before Higgins's death, at the age of forty-five, in 1941.

Unfortunately, in James P. McGlone's biography of Ria Mooney, Kavanagh's name is mentioned only once and then in a general context as one of three writers (the others were Flann O'Brien and Brendan Behan) who were 'condemned to penury, or finally forced to employ eccentricity, showmanship and bravado in order to attract the attention of the English and American public'. O'Brien, of course, had been the private secretary to a number of government Ministers and was not penurious, nor, though he was an alcoholic, did he put on a stage Irishman act for anyone. Behan certainly played the part, largely because he was a natural performer. Kavanagh, however, had a horror of playing the Paddy and satirized the type in 'The Paddiad', which was written in, or shortly before, 1949. Of course, he was an extraordinarily large personality, quite capable of behaving outrageously, but, as Elizabeth O'Toole's memoir shows, he was also capable of living in a house with two highly educated and, in the social sense, respectable adults, and four children, who were very fond of him. This is also true of his relationship with Senator Joan Ryan, wife of Eoin, then Vice-President of Fianna Fáil, and a host of other people, mainly women. As Quinn puts it,

'For all his railings against the bourgeoisie, Kavanagh's caring, forgiving, unconditionally loving God is envisaged as not only maternal, but middle-class.'

According to Antoinette Quinn's biography, Kavanagh spent Christmas 1960 with his future wife Katherine Moloney in her Gibson Square flat in Islington and returned to Dublin at the end of January 1961 to give his annual lectures in UCD. But, according to Elizabeth O'Toole's memoir, he arrived in Stillorgan on St Stephen's Day, spitting blood, which alarmed Elizabeth so much she wanted him brought to hospital. The fact that he was wet suggests that he had been out in the rain and was perhaps exhausted by travelling all day from London by train and boat.

According to Quinn, however, Kavanagh did not return from London until the end of January 1961 when he moved to a flat in Haddington Road, staying there until March. Elizabeth O'Toole refers to the flat but says Kavanagh asked Jim O'Toole to fetch from it things he needed, including, remarkably, his cobbler's tools – which Elizabeth saw him using in Priory Grove. How he could have arranged for the tools to be in a short-term flat in Haddington Road is baffling, unless he somehow organized it from London before Christmas, either by letter or, much more difficult in those days, by a long-distance, operator-assisted phone call.

Elizabeth O'Toole's account of Kavanagh's recovery, of her own tetchiness at being addressed as 'Woman' – thereafter he called her Betty – and of his crying as he helped her hang out her washing, is so vivid that it must be true; but the continuity of the narrative, a writerly device, does not exclude the likelihood that as Kavanagh's health improved, he went into town to do business. The device may also explain why the memoir makes no mention of what was the most pressing matter on Elizabeth's mind: the rehearsals for *Man Alive!*, which opened on 21 January.

The Quinn biography says that the poet was evicted from the Haddington Road flat on 1 March 1961 'for some unspecified damage to the property', but it is by no means clear which flat this was: Quinn says he had been 'given the run' of several flats in the area.[63] A similar vagueness arises from her report that Kavanagh had found a room to rent in the area, at 37 Upper Mount Street, 'from May 1961 onwards'. There can be no doubt that he did rent this 'damp room at the end of a corridor' and that he stayed there 'on and off' for the next four years, but there is considerable doubt about the beginning of the period. It seems that at this time the elderly owner of the flat, Violet McWeeney, was sharing it with the poet Leland Bardwell (1922–2016), the latter's partner Fintan McLachlan, and numerous children. In any event, probably by the middle of that year, the Bardwell ménage moved from Upper Mount Street just around the corner to a basement flat at 33 Lower Leeson Street, which is the scene of almost all Leland's anecdotes of Kavanagh.[64]

By her own account, Bardwell's life was 'a crescendo of madness', and these years, switching back and forth between Ireland and England, were chaotic.[65] It is likely, therefore, that in 1961 Kavanagh was using the Upper Mount Street room only when he was in town while living in Stillorgan, which was then still a village on the outskirts of the city with a poor bus service.

Quinn herself describes Kavanagh as 'Leland's guest', not a tenant paying rent. Bearing out Margot O'Toole's account, Quinn quotes Leland saying that 'she was despatched every morning to fetch a naggin of whiskey (the hair of the dog), without which he could not start the day.' In itself, this raises the issue of Kavanagh's alcoholism and frequent episodes of extreme drunkenness. If that had been the case in the O'Toole household, where there were four young children, one of them, Jacqueline, with a heart condition, it is unlikely that their abstemious mother would have put up with it.

Quinn also says that Kavanagh was in poor health that summer, quoting a letter Patrick wrote to Peter in New York in August, in which he says he thought his illness was 'psychosomatic'. Capacious though that term is, it hardly allows for a sick man being fit enough to go swimming in the sea at Greystones, as described in the memoir, nor for the man who was, when he began living in London with Katherine Moloney that August, 'in great form'.[66] Nor does his drinking, even if he was a highly functioning alcoholic, easily accommodate the active freelance journalist, the UCD lecturer, the Guinness Award judge, the libretto writer, and the poet operating at the height of his powers, which Kavanagh still was in 1961.

According to the Quinn biography, Kavanagh opened an account 'with the Chancery Lane and Holborn branch of the Westminster Bank at the beginning of February', which 'indicated his identification of himself as a Londoner at this period'. The biography also records Patrick Swift, the outstanding Irish artist, painting Kavanagh's portrait in Katherine Moloney's flat in Gibson Square, which would in itself have been inconvenient because it is almost a half-an-hour journey by Tube from the Chancery Lane bank. In the Quinn biography, Swift's daughter Kate recalls how she and her father 'found the poet in a low bed pushed against the wall and covered with an army blanket' and that when he was awakened he 'immediately' asked her father 'to spread some newspapers beside the bed and proceeded to retch and vomit.'

While there is no reason to doubt this vivid memory, there is a problem with when and where it happened, not least because Katherine Moloney was a house-proud and orderly person. The biography says that Swift 'was painting the portrait at the start of 1961' and that Kavanagh opened his bank account in February, but it also says that he 'had to return to Dublin to give his UCD lectures' at 'the end of January'; that he moved into a flat on Haddington Road, described as 'a short-lived tenancy'; that he was evicted on 1 March for causing 'some unspecified damage to the property'; that he was 'given the run' from several flats in the area, usually for non-payment of rent, 'or the squalor in which he lived'; and that on one occasion he was evicted because of 'a bad smell which was traced to his stash of unwashed socks'. Oddly enough, the detail about the socks is borne out by the memoir, where Elizabeth records Jim O'Toole going to the Haddington Road flat to fetch some of Kavanagh's things, including his cobbler's last, but deciding that the socks were too worn out to be saved. The problem yet again is the timing: Quinn's information came from two letters to her written by Noel Henry in December 1997 and January 1998. Kavanagh was very friendly with Frank Henry, a retired schoolteacher from Mayo, and his sons Leo and Maurice, the latter a journalist with the Irish Cooperative Society, but who Noel Henry was is not known.

At a distance of almost sixty years, the difficulties of establishing the dates of Kavanagh's stay in Stillorgan are considerable, but the examination of the details here, following discussions with Margot O'Toole and her family, leads to the conclusion that he arrived not on Stephen's Day 1960, or during the period leading up to the premiere of *Man Alive!* on 21 January 1961, but shortly afterwards, either by the end of that month or the beginning of February; and that he stayed with the family until sometime in the summer.

Kavanagh stayed in touch with the O'Tooles after he had left Stillorgan. Elizabeth remembers that when he attended the party held for her husband before Jim went to teach at Ohio State University in 1964, Paddy spent much of the night sitting on the stairs talking to her eight-year-old daughter EllyMay. That was typical of him. In poetry, it was the child-like vision he had seen in Inniskeen in 1910 that he sought to return to, when his 'father played the melodion' and the poet was 'six Christmases of age'. Fifty years later, although he was still a comparatively young man, he could have said without self-pity that life had, in Richard Murphy's words, given him 'the bum's rush in the dark': the indignity of being thrown into the canal was merely a bathetic addition to the misery of his financial insecurity and ill-health, both of which were chronic.

What he got in Priory Grove, as well as a temporary refuge and the care and sympathy of adults, came to him from the O'Toole children: through them he could revisit the vision of his original Christmas childhood, the memory of a time when 'it was actually earlier/ Than many people thought'.

Elizabeth O'Toole, or Betty as the poet called her, gives no indication of having read Antoinette Quinn's biography, neither countering it nor relying on it, as readers do now and will continue to do in future, but with added reservations. In this editor's opinion, the dating of events in both the biography and the memoir, as well as the nature of Kavanagh's alcoholism, of his boorishness, of his reticence, even secretiveness, and of his relationships with women, particularly with Patricia Avis, merit reconsideration.

Should there be such a reconsideration, it will owe a good deal to something that is not of primary concern to Elizabeth O'Toole: the revelation of her own character as an individual and as a representative of her class in mid-twentieth-century Ireland. Not only was she kind in the sense of sympathy, she was independent, high-minded, not to be trifled with, capable, spiritual, a lover of literature and a friend to the poet. When, in his old-fashioned way, Kavanagh addressed her as 'Woman' he also meant this:

> Surely my God is feminine, for Heaven
> Is the generous impulse, is contented
> With feeding praise to the good. And all
> Of these that I have known have come from women.
> While men the poet's tragic light resented,
> The spirit that is Woman caressed his soul.[67]

Elizabeth M. Ryan O'Toole's family

COMPILED BY MARGOT O'TOOLE

Elizabeth Ryan, born 7 September 1924, Ballymorris House, Cratloe, Co. Clare

1930–36 Primary education: Cratloe National School,

1936–42 Secondary education: Laurel Hill Convent, Limerick

1942–7 Further education: Cathal Brugha Street College, Dublin Institute of Technology, Culinary Arts and Food Technology. Degrees in Nutritional Science and Home Economics Education. Extra year of training in institutional administration and management.

1947–8 Teacher in Drishane Convent, Co. Cork.

1949–51 Lecturer, Church of Ireland College of Education, Dublin.

1949–56 Lecturer, Dundrum Technical School, Ballsbridge Technical School, and Cathal Brugha Street College.

1969–72 Simmons College, Boston, Massachussets.

1967–92 Teacher, Home Arts and Science, Public Schools, Brookline, Massachussetts, USA.
Exhibition, Marion Arts Center, Boston – 'Paintings by Elizabeth O'Toole', August 2015.

Marriage: 28 August 1949 to James Davitt Bermingham O'Toole.

Children: Laurence Paul Claudel (Larry), 1950; Margaret Mary (Margot), 1952; EllyMay, 1955; Jacqueline Marty (Jaja), 1958.

Parents: Laurence Ryan, farmer, thoroughbred horse breeder, Justice of the Peace, and Helen Mary (May) Watson, of County Cork, businesswoman, pianist, trained in culinary arts.

Brothers: Robert (deceased) doctor, practised in Wolverhampton, England; Jack (deceased) doctor, practised in Limerick; Laurence (deceased) Director of Irish National Stud (Kildare); Thomas (deceased) farmer and poet, County Limerick.

Sisters: Marjorie Ryan Harvey, former dress designer and leading member of the Irish Countrywomen's Association; Kathleen (Kitty) Ryan MacGabhann (deceased) social worker, former proprietor Children's Shop, Limerick.

Notes

A POET IN THE HOUSE

1. When the author was a student in Dublin, she made an unsuccessful attempt to arrange to have Patrick Kavanagh give a guest lecture at Laurel Hill.

2. Kathleen Ryan appeared in many films, at least one of which is a classic: *Odd Man Out* directed by Carol Reed. Her family owned the Monument Creameries, a chain of thirty-three shops, and her brother, John, the editor of *Envoy*, was close to Kavanagh.

3. Both sides of the O'Toole family were friendly with Dr Hillery. Margot O'Toole remembers meeting him in Kilkee, County Clare, when she was a child, and that he came to her grandfather's hundredth birthday celebration. Margot O'Toole, email to the editor, 20 December 2019.

4. Anthony Raftery or Antoine Ó Raifteirí (1779–1835) was a blind poet who wrote in Irish and was one of the last wandering bards.

5. John Charles McQuaid (1895–1973) was born in Cootehill, County Cavan and became Archbishop in 1940.

6. As of 2021, despite great changes to the village of Stillorgan, 'Nimble Fingers' is still in business. The first bowling alley and the first shopping centre in Ireland were built in Stillorgan in 1963 and 1966 respectively.

7. This is an interesting example of how Elizabeth O'Toole either memorized or transcribed the poem. As editor, I have added to her text the final line as it appears in the *Collected Poems*; that version begins 'O God' whereas her version begins 'Great God'. I have also silently corrected the title, which Mrs O'Toole remembers as 'To Anna Quinn', which is what it is called in the Patrick Kavanagh Trust version. That version ends thus: 'The loveliness of earth? the girls that pass'.

8. 'Stickyback' is one of many common names in Ireland for Galium aparine.

9. *Collected Poems*, ed. Antoinette Quinn (London: Penguin UK, 2005), p. 229. Hereafter Quinn, *CP*.

10. Born in Limerick, Gerald Griffin (1803–40) was a successful novelist and playwright, the author of *The Colleen Bawn*. On joining the Christian Brothers in 1838, he burned all his manuscripts, but died of typhus two years later.

11. At this time the place was 'Gentlemen Only', but in 1974 women invaded and asserted their right to swim there too. The Forty Foot features in the first chapter of James Joyce's *Ulysses*. The distance to Dun Laoghaire pier is about half a mile as the crow swims.

12. Punchestown, in County Kildare, holds a Festival in April, the Irish equivalent of the Cheltenham Festival in England. The Harty family are famous horse trainers over fences and Vincent O'Brien was the leading trainer over the flat. 'Martin Molony is up' is a colloquialism meaning he was the jockey.

13. Here the author misremembers in an interesting way: Kavanagh was referring to 1924 when Mabel Young fell in love with Paul Henry. She left him when she discovered that he was married, but they married in 1954 after his wife, Grace, died. Paul Henry died on 28 August 1958. One particular stand of trees by the road between Dublin and Punchestown was said to have served as the inspiration

for one of Mabel Young's beech tree paintings. Carn Lake in County Cavan was another of Young's favourite subjects.

14. 'The Lark in the Clear Air' by Sir Samuel Ferguson (1810–86).

15. Maggie Men used to be common at race meetings and fairs: one man sold clubs to onlookers who then threw them at a man in a barrel. Jack B. Yeats painted the subject twice; in Cathal Black's film, *Love and Rage*, scripted by this editor, the first scene features old-style Maggie Men. By the 1950s Maggie Men were selling trinkets.

16. '*Deas*' is the word in the Irish language for 'pretty'. The child, at an age when she was learning the Irish language, was emphasizing that the items on the cart are very pretty, using an English/Irish hybrid word.

17. Probably a cheap version of a Claddagh Bell, an item still sold in souvenir shops.

18. In the 1950s there was a popular line of clockwork Peter Rabbit toys. Flopsy, Mopsy and Cottontail were Peter's siblings.

19. This was a little, blue rubber dolly with a right elbow bent up and the palm facing forward. The hand position mimicked the one used by children at school when asking permission to go to the bathroom. '*An bhfuil cead agam dul go dtí an leithreas?*', translates as 'Do I have permission to go to the lavatory?' EllyMay named the doll Cead Agam on the spot, very much to Paddy's amusement.

20. An Irish variation of 'gewgaws', an English word of uncertain origin, meaning trinkets.

21. 'Half a crown' was a coin worth two shillings and sixpence; a 'bob' was a shilling; so 'five bob' was two half-crowns. There were eight half-crowns to a pound.

22. From 'Street Corner Christ', Patrick Kavanagh, July 1938.

23. Miniature bowling pins, which are still being sold.

24. Jack Yellen (1892–1991) wrote the lyrics and Milton Ager (1893–1979) the music for the song in 1929.

25. The reference is to Father P.J. McGrath, who eventually left the priesthood and brought a significant case to the High Court against St Patrick's College, Maynooth.

26. According to Margot O'Toole, her father's interest in de Chardin's views on evolution led to her own fascination with biology and her career in science. From an email to the editor, 20 December 2019.

27. A Scottish nursery rhyme. Stousie refers to a small child who cannot run on its own.

28. According to Margot O'Toole, they came to the house because her mother was 'a great scholar of Irish literature … The Christian Brothers were teaching Irish, and she was helping them and allowing them to review her resources'. From an email to the editor, 20 February 2019.

29. The couple lived in the seaside village of Dalkey, County Dublin, but Jack was 'a high-spirited man in every sense of the word'. Movita, seeking a quieter life, went back to America and married Marlon Brando. Michael Taub, *Jack Doyle: the Gorgeous Gael* (Dublin: The Lilliput Press, 2007; 2nd ed.)

30. See Patrick Walsh, *Patrick Kavanagh and* The Leader: *The Poet, the Politician and the Libel Trial* (Cork: Mercier Press, 2010).

31. John O'Toole had held a series of senior positions, including Assistant Commissioner, in the Shanghai Municipal Police. For a description of his career, see Timothy G. McMahon, Michael de Nie, and Paul Townend (eds), *Ireland in an Imperial World: Citizenship, Opportunism, and Subversion* (London: Springer, 2017).

32. The Collège Municipal was built in 1917 and operated by the Alliance Française.

33. There is an entry on Patrick Bermingham in Wikipedia.

34. There was a strong tradition of resistance and activism on both sides of Jimmy O'Toole's family. His mother, Elly (Bermingham) O'Toole, was evicted from her home in

Moyasta, County Clare as a very young child. The bonds between the Berminghams and the descendants of those who took them in after that eviction remain strong to this day.

35. Both the O'Toole and Bermingham families were involved in the Land League, an Irish agrarian organization that worked for the reform of the landlord system. The League was founded in October 1879 by Michael Davitt, the son of an evicted tenant farmer.

36. Agnes McGowan married Colonel Francis Hayley Bell, a Boer War veteran, who served in the Chinese Maritime Custom Service in Shanghai. Their daughter, Mary Hayley Bell, was born there. The O'Tooles and the Hayley Bells remained friendly.

37. This was quite a feat of memory: the poem is 288 lines long.

38. Bull's-eyes were hard, ball-shaped, striped black and white candies. Gur cake is a confection associated with Dublin, sometimes made by using whiskey to hold together a mixture of leftover cake crumbs and dried fruit.

39. Maureen Potter was a comedian. 'Even the poet Patrick Kavanagh, as the grumpiest man in Dublin, once walked up to her and said: "Do you know what? You're not a bad little woman at all".' Stephen Dixon, 'Maureen Potter: Ireland's Variety Heroine Who Trod the Boards for 70 Years', *The Guardian*, 13 April 2004.

40. For a discussion of the innumerable versions of this story, see the Afterword. The woman unnamed in the story, Patricia Avis, was well known to Kavanagh.

41. The spellings have been left as they are in the original manuscript. The Afterword identifies the poem. Since Elizabeth's Irish is very good, the errors are probably due to the transcription of her handwriting in the United States.

42. Patrick's sister Celia entered the Presentation Convent in Matlock, Derbyshire in August 1933.

43. According to Bernard Share in *Slanguage: Dictionary of Irish Slang* (Dublin: Gill and Macmillan, 1997), a 'coldoy' is a bad halfpenny; a worthless article.

44. Elizabeth O'Toole is remembering the poem beginning 'On an apple-ripe September morning'. Three stanzas appeared in Kavanagh's 'City Commentary' column in the *Irish Press* on 27 September 1943 entitled 'A Reverie of Poor Piers'. A longer version appears in *Tarry Flynn* (London: Pilot Press, 1948), pp. 188–9. In Quinn, *CP*, the eight-stanza poem is entitled 'Threshing Morning', pp. 112–13.

45. Quinn, *CP*, p. 229.

46. From 'Inniskeen Road: July Evening', Quinn, *CP*, p. 15.

PATRICK KAVANAGH AT PRIORY GROVE

1. Notes by the author are identified in situ; otherwise they are by the editor.

2. Una Agnew, *The Mystical Imagination of Patrick Kavanagh* (Dublin: Columba Press, 1998; Dublin: Veritas, 2019 [revd. ed.]), p. 39, and, in the 2019 edition, p. 57.

3. Antoinette Quinn, *Patrick Kavanagh, A Biography* (Dublin: Gill and Macmillan, 2002), p. 344; hereafter referred to as Quinn, *Biography*.

4. *Patrick Kavanagh: Collected Poems* (London: Martin Brian & O'Keeffe, 1964), p. 143.

5. Ibid, p. 70

6. Quinn, *Biography*, p. 315.

7. Alma Holgersen (1899–1976) was Austrian. The poem was published in Vienna in 1965 in a collection called *Ein Reh zu Gast*.

8. The university was founded in 1903 by Joseph Ma Xiangbo, S.J. In 1905 Ma resigned to establish Fudan University, and Aurora was thereafter run by French Jesuits until the

Communist Revolution took it over in 1952. From 1908 onwards it was located in Shanghai's French Concession.

9. This information comes from his correspondence. Waag, now known as Nové Mesto nad Váhom, or in German as Neustadt an der Waag, is a town in the Trenčín Region of Slovakia.

10. David O'Donoghue, 'New Evidence on IRA/Nazi Links, *History Ireland*, vol. 19, no. 2 (2011); David O'Donoghue, *The Devil's Deal: The IRA, Nazi Germany and the Double Life of Jim O'Donovan* (Dublin: New Island Books, 2010); J. Bowyer Bell, *The Secret Army: The IRA* (Wallingford, Oxfordshire: Routledge, 1997).

11. This note and the following supplied by the author: Information on issuance comes from replacement passport and visa, and dates of travel in old passports. Information on his stop in London comes from Michael Hayes.

12. The police were observed by Michael Hayes, who lived in the house for many years, starting in 1942. It was explained to Michael by other occupants and neighbours that the police were there to watch over Jimmy.

13. Author's note: Information from Michael Hayes, who attended the championship match.

14. The Dundalk-born Paul Vincent Carroll (1900–68) was a friend of Kavanagh. *Shadow and Substance* won the New York Drama Critics Circle award for best foreign play in 1937.

15. Author's note: I remember that Erskine Childers was one of the commentators. There were others whose names I do not remember. I remember my father commenting on situations in the Congo and in Algeria.

16. Ernest Blythe, letter to James O'Toole, dated 3 November 1958.

17. Godfrey Quigley (1923–94), who had trained at the Abbey, went on to appear in Stanley Kubrick's *Clockwork Orange* (1971) and *Barry Lyndon* (1975).

18. Fitzgerald died in 2003. Playwright Tom Kilroy describes him in his memoir, *Over the Backyard Wall* (Dublin: The Lilliput Press,

2019); and his work is discussed in Nicholas Grene, Patrick Lonergan, and Lilian Chambers (eds), *Interactions: Dublin Theatre Festival*, 1957–2007 (Dublin: Carysfort Press, 2008).

19. Author's note: The people at Seapoint always called my dad 'Mac'. I don't know why. I never heard him called Mac anywhere else; he seemed to accept without comment and with good humour that, while at Seapoint, his name was Mac.

A POET IN THE HOUSE: AN AFTERWORD

1. Quinn, *Biography*, p. 331.

2. Although *Man Alive!* was, according to Elizabeth O'Toole, 'slammed' by Patrick O'Connor in 'Chronicle, Theatre' in a Catholic journal, *The Furrow*, vol. 12, no. 3 (March 1961), pp. 174–6, other notices were good, including one by John Jordan, in *Hibernia Fortnightly Review*. Jordan was a lecturer in University College Dublin, a short story writer, a poet, an eminent critic, and one of Kavanagh's closest friends.

3. The play was published under the title *Man Alive!, A play* by James O'Toole (Dublin: Allen Figgis, 1962).

4. The website, 'Playography Ireland, a comprehensive database of new Irish plays produced professionally since 1904' contains the complete programme plus details of cast members.

5. Information kindly supplied to the editor by the ESB's archivist Tanya Keyes.

6. It is unlikely that what is meant is the Jewish Conservatory of Music, founded in 1927, but there were many Jewish schools in Shanghai. See Jonathan Goldstein (ed.), *The Jews of China* (Armonk, New York: M.E. Sharpe, 1998), p. 231.

7. The firm of J. Watson in Youghal was central to the stained-glass industry in Ireland, but it is not known if they had any connection to the Watsons in Charleville. See Finola Finlay,

'Watsons of Youghal, Revivalist Masters Part 1', *Roaring Water Journal*, 13 October 2019.

8. The College was opened officially in 1941 by the Archbishop of Dublin, John Charles McQuaid, who, as the memoir records, was Kavanagh's patron.

9. The other children are Margaret Mary (Margot), born in June 1952, a scientist; EllyMay (Helena Mary), born in August 1955, scientist and teacher; and Jacqueline (Jaja), born in February 1958. Larry's career as a businessman and philanthropist is well documented on social media.

10. RIC Constables were officially known as 'Candidates' until they were 27. Although sons of RIC men were allowed to join the force earlier than others, if John did spend two years in Paris, he could only have joined the RIC, very briefly, at the age of 19 or 20. See Jim Herlihy, *The Royal Irish Constabulary* (Dublin: Four Courts Press, 2016), p. 85.

11. See C. W. Sullivan III, 'Reconsidering the Convict Ships', *New Hibernia Review*, vol. 12, no. 4 (Winter 2008), pp. 101–16.

12. As late as 1882, the Fenian 'Invincibles' assassinated the Chief Secretary for Ireland, Frederick Cavendish, and his Permanent Under-Secretary, Thomas Henry Burke, in the Phoenix Park in Dublin.

13. For information on how the Shanghai police recruited in London, see the Wikipedia entry on the Shanghai Municipal Police. The force also had close connections to France, so it is quite possible that John O'Toole was recruited in Paris.

14. The quote and much of the information in this paragraph comes from the extraordinarily detailed blog of Paddy Waldron at http://pwaldron.info/genealogy/shanghai.htm.

15. See the photograph by Robert French, 'T. Birmingham's house, Moyasta, Co. Clare with Battering Ram', in the National Library's Lawrence Collection. The evictions were long foreseen: Fenian sympathizers came over from New

York to witness the events. See Frank McNally, 'Blunt instrument – the Kilrush evictions of 1888 and the "Vandeleur ram"', *The Irish Times*, 5 July 2019, and Ed O'Shaughnessy, 'Officials from the Vandeleur Evictions', *The Other Clare*, vol. 42 (2018), pp. 54–60.

16. See Patsy McGarry, 'We have already commemorated the RIC – 10 years ago', *The Irish Times*, 17 January 2020.

17. It is possible that O'Toole, on his way back from Shanghai to Ireland, heard him lecture in Paris.

18. The passport and the visa are in the possession of the O'Toole family.

19. Margot writes: 'This information is based on what my father told Michael Hayes at the time.'

20. As it happens, this editor wrote a 4-part TV drama about those spies, *Caught in a Free State*, directed by Peter Ormrod and broadcast by RTÉ and by Channel 4 in England in 1984.

21. Also on board was Frank Ryan, the socialist revolutionary. For a brief view of the Nazi–IRA relationship, see Brian Hanley, 'Oh, Here's to Adolf Hitler?'…The IRA and the Nazis', *History Ireland*, vol. 13, no. 3 (May/June 2005).

22. See Owen McCrohan, *Paddy Mo – the Life of Patrick Moriarty 1926–1997* (Dublin: The Lilliput Press, 2008).

23. For a 2004 profile by her friends the poets Eiléan Ní Chuilleanáin and Macdara Woods, see 'Poetry, politics, friendship and fun', *The Irish Times*, 16 October 2004. This editor was a friend of Katherine.

24. The only full-length biography of Barry was written by Monty and Jim's son, Donal O'Donovan, and is entitled *Kevin Barry and His Time* (Dublin: Glendale, 1998).

25. See David O'Donoghue, *The Devil's Deal: The IRA, Nazi Germany and the Double Life of Jim O'Donovan* (Dublin: New Island Books, 2010), p. 69. There is no mention of Jim O'Toole in the book.

26. As well as recruiting George Furlong, Director of the National Gallery, as an agent, Betjeman specialized in spreading rumours, known as 'sibs' in the intelligence community. For the term, see https://sites.durham.ac.uk/writersandpropaganda /tag/siboftheweek/.

27. *CP*, pp. 266–70. See also Quinn, *Biography*, p. 351.

28. See Quinn, *Biography*, p. 371. See also an anecdote witnessed by Tommy O'Keefe in 1961, when Kavanagh, probably while he was living in Stillorgan, described Behan in Mooney's pub in Baggot Street as 'a pig': Tommy O'Keeffe, 'Overheard on Baggot Street: An exchange between Patrick Kavanagh and Brendan Behan', *The Irish Times*, 10 May 2019.

29. Tierney and O'Donovan were students in UCD and joined the IRA together. See O'Donoghue, *The Devil's Deal*, p. 5.

30. The nearest approach to the truth is probably to be found in a letter from Owen Dwyer entitled 'Kavanagh in the Canal' in *The Irish Times* (10 November 2005), making allowances for the fact that Owen's father, Dinny, was rumoured to be one of the perpetrators. See also Quinn, *Biography*, p. 384 et seq.

31. Quinn, *Biography*, p. 386.

32. Patricia Avis, *Playing the Harlot or Mostly Coffee* (London: Virago Modern Classics Series, 1996, with an introduction by George H. Gilpin and Hermione de Almeida of the University of Tulsa, Oklahoma). See also Richard Murphy's autobiography, *The Kick: A Memoir* (London: Granta Books, 2002).

33. Emily is the mother of the well-known YouTube vlogger Caspar Lee.

34. For a list of the contributions, which includes the title poem of the book, *Come Dance with Kitty Stobling and Other Poems* (London: Longmans, 1960), see Quinn, *Biography*, p. 386.

35. Hogan also contributed a review of a book on Antonin Artaud. It is noteworthy, as will be seen, that when Artaud came to Dublin in 1937, he contacted Adolph Mahr, Director of the

National Museum and a prominent Nazi. For an account of Artaud, described by an Irish diplomat as 'travelling light in the upper storey', see Antonin Artaud, 'An absent-minded person of the student type', *The Dublin Review*, No. 1, Winter 2000–1.

36. 'Winter', Quinn, *CP*, p. 232.

37. Peter Kavanagh, *Sacred Keeper: A Biography of Patrick Kavanagh* (County Kildare, The Curragh: The Goldsmith Press, 1979).

38. As editor in charge of the Faber poetry list, Monteith would later be Seamus Heaney's publisher.

39. See 'T. Desmond Williams (1921–87)', an obituary by James McGuire, *Irish Historical Studies*, vol. 26, no. 101 (May 1988).

40. See the biography of Kerney by Barry Whelan, entitled *Ireland's Revolutionary Diplomat: A Biography of Leopold Kerney* (Notre Dame, Indiana: Notre Dame University Press, 2019).

41. Quinn, *Biography*, p. 316, says there is now 'a general consensus' that Iremonger was responsible. Bridget Hourican states it as a fact in her entry on him in James McGuire and James Quinn (eds), *Dictionary of Irish Biography: from the Earliest Times to the Year 2002* (Cambridge: Cambridge University Press, 2009).

42. It was not at all unusual in the IRA to be, as O'Donovan was, a Nazi sympathizer and a supporter of the communist side in the Spanish Civil War. In 2003 Mary Lou McDonald marked the beginning of her career in Sinn Féin, of which she became President in 2018, by speaking at a memorial to the Nazi collaborator and IRA Chief of Staff Seán Russell.

43. In an interview in America in 1957, Kavanagh said, 'I'd hate to appear anti-semitic. But they [Jews] influence American literature completely.' In the same interview he said of J.D. Salinger. 'I think he's Jewish thrash [*sic*]. He's the perfect thrash.' The US literary establishment he described as 'a sort of left wing and it derives from the '30s in England, the pink '30s and they've never advanced

beyond the Spanish Civil War.' For a facsimile of the typed document, see the UCD cultural collections website at https://ucdculturalheritagecollections.com/2017/11/16/mr-kavanagh-goes-to-america/#jp-carousel-1425.

44. See Eunan O'Halpin, *Spying on Ireland: British Intelligence and Irish Neutrality During the Second World War* (Oxford: Oxford University Press, 2010), p. 52. O'Halpin is the nephew of Katherine Moloney, Patrick Kavanagh's wife.

45. There were a number of other Germans who could have tried to recruit O'Toole in Berlin: Oscar Pfaus and Franz Fromme, for example, and in Dublin there were Nazi sympathizers, like Adolf Mahr, who was appointed director of the National Museum of Ireland in 1934, and took indefinite unpaid leave from that position in 1939. See Gerry Mullins, *Dublin Nazi No. 1: The Life of Adolf Mahr* (Dublin: Liberties Press, 2007).

46. See Peter Kavanagh, *Patrick Kavanagh: A Life Chronicle* (New York: Peter Kavanagh Hand Press, c. 2000), pp. 311–12.

47. 'The Same Again', Quinn, *CP*, pp. 245–6. For a description of Kavanagh's use of baking powder as a cure, see John McGahern's short story 'My Love, My Umbrella', *Nightlines* (London: Faber, 1970).

48. Unless otherwise stated, the information about Doyle comes from *Michael Taub, Jack Doyle: the Gorgeous Gael* (Dublin: The Lilliput Press, 2007; 2nd ed.). Taub quotes the Doyle verse from Peter Kavanagh (ed.), *Patrick Kavanagh: The Complete Poems* (County Kildare, The Curragh: The Goldsmith Press, 1972).

49. The punctuation is supplied by the editor. Kavanagh would certainly have been aware that the last line is unmetrical, but either he was content to leave it like that or, more likely, the version we have is a draft found in his papers. The poem is quoted in Taub.

50. Taub records him being knocked out in the first round of a fight held in Dalymount Park, the soccer stadium in Phibsborough, Dublin. Most reports say Doyle was too drunk to stand up,

but Movita says he was drugged by gamblers to make sure he wouldn't win.

51. Patrick Kavanagh, 'The Gambler: A Ballet', *Collected Poems* (London: MacGibbon and Kee, 1964), pp. 176–8.

52. Quinn's endnote reads: 'PK to Jim O'Toole, 4 April 1961, copy or unposted letter in KA' (the Kavanagh archive in UCD).

53. Almost all Kavanagh's letters in this UCD folder are typed carbon copies of the original. This one is signed in ink.

54. Patrick O'Connor, 'Chronicle, Theatre', *The Furrow*, vol. 12, no. 3 (March 1961), pp. 174–6.

55. For O'Connor's role in the notorious sale of paintings by Guardi, see Peter Murray, 'Crusades in Art', *Irish Arts Review*, 27 March 2015.

56. Quinn, *Biography*, p. 331.

57. Dr Lawlor died in 2018 in her ninety-seventh year. The closeness of the families is indicated by the fact that her husband, Arthur, who predeceased her, worked in the ESB. For an appreciation of him and his work as an engineer and the inventor of the 'convector heater', see T.L., 'An Appreciation: Arthur Lawlor', *The Irish Times*, 10 January 2005.

58. Quinn, *Biography*, p. 322 and endnote.

59. Quinn, *Biography*, p. 376. The quoted words come from his column in the *Irish Farmers Journal*, 22 November 1958.

60. 'Literary Adventures', Quinn, *CP*, pp. 241–2.

61. Larry Sheedy, *That's Another Story: a Miscellany of Traveller's Tales* [*sic*] (Blackrock, Dublin: Irish Food Publishers, 1993). Dun Laoghaire public library note states that 'these stories were originally written for and broadcast on RTÉ Radio One's programme Sunday Miscellany.'

62. Ann Marie Hourihane, 'The many faces of TP McKenna', *The Irish Times*, 19 February 2011.

63. This detail is from Quinn, *Biography*, p. 400. The 1960/61 period is examined in pp. 398–403, but there is a degree of crossover in the coverage of earlier and later events.

64. This editor was in the Leeson Street flat on a number of occasions from 1964 onwards but never met Kavanagh there.

65. See the anonymous 'Obituary: Leland Bardwell', *Sunday Independent*, 3 July 2016; and Richard Pine, 'Leland Bardwell Obituary', *The Guardian*, 24 July 2016.

66. It was at this time that Kavanagh's friend, Patrick Swift painted a powerful portrait of the poet. See http://painterpatrick-swift.blogspot.com/2009/11/patrick-kavanagh-section.html. The website contains invaluable information about Swift and Kavanagh: see also, for example, the entry on the writer John McGahern.

67. 'God in Woman', *Collected Poems* (1964), p. 147

Select Bibliography

Agnew, Una, *The Mystical Imagination of Patrick Kavanagh* (Dublin: Columba Press, 1998; Dublin: Veritas, 2019 [revd. ed.])

Avis, Patricia, *Playing the Harlot or Mostly Coffee* (London: Virago Modern Classics Series, 1996)

Bowyer Bell J., *The Secret Army: The IRA* (Wallingford, Oxfordshire: Routledge, 1997)

Goldstein, Jonathan (ed.), *The Jews of China* (Armonk, New York: M.E. Sharpe, 1998)

Grene, Nicholas, Patrick Lonergan and Lilian Chambers (eds), *Interactions: Dublin Theatre Festival, 1957–2007,* (Dublin: Carysfort Press, 2008)

Herlihy, Jim, *The Royal Irish Constabulary* (Dublin: Four Courts Press, 2016)

Kavanagh, Patrick*, Patrick Kavanagh: Collected Poems* (London: Martin Brian & O'Keeffe, 1964)

———, 'The Gambler: A Ballet', *Collected Poems* (London: MacGibbon and Kee, 1964)

———, *Tarry Flynn* (London: Four Square, an imprint of the New English Library, 1962)

Kavanagh, Peter (ed.), *Patrick Kavanagh: The Complete Poems* (County Kildare, The Curragh: The Goldsmith Press, 1972)

———, *Patrick Kavanagh: A Life Chronicle* (New York: Peter Kavanagh Hand Press, c. 2000)

———, *Sacred Keeper: A Biography of Patrick Kavanagh* (County Kildare: The Curragh, The Goldsmith Press, 1979)

Kilroy, Tom, *Over the Backyard Wall* (Dublin: The Lilliput Press, 2019)

McCrohan, Owen, *Paddy Mo – the Life of Patrick Moriarty 1926–1997* (Dublin: The Lilliput Press, 2008)

McGahern, John, *Nightlines* (London: Faber, 1970)

McGuire, James and Quinn, James (eds), *Dictionary of Irish Biography: from the Earliest Times to the Year 2002* (Cambridge: Cambridge University Press, 2009)

McMahon Timothy G., Michael de Nie, and Paul Townend (eds), *Ireland in an Imperial World: Citizenship, Opportunism, and Subversion* (London: Springer, 2017)

Mullins, Gerry, *Dublin Nazi No. 1: The Life of Adolf Mahr* (Dublin: Liberties Press, 2007)

Murphy, Richard, *The Kick: A Memoir* (London: Granta Books, 2002)

O'Donoghue, David, *The Devil's Deal: The IRA, Nazi Germany and the Double Life of Jim O'Donovan* (Dublin: New Island Books, 2010)

O'Donovan, Donal, *Kevin Barry and his Time* (Dublin: Glendale, 1998)

O'Faolain, Julia, *Trespassers – A Memoir* (London: Faber & Faber, 2013)

O'Halpin, Eunan, *Spying on Ireland: British Intelligence and Irish Neutrality During the Second World War* (Oxford: Oxford University Press, 2010)

O'Toole, James, *Man Alive!, play in three acts* (Dublin: Allen Figgis, 1962)

Quinn, Antoinette (ed.), *Patrick Kavanagh: Collected Poems* (London: Penguin Modern Classics, 2005)

—, *Patrick Kavanagh, A Biography* (Dublin: Gill and Macmillan, 2002)

Share, Bernard, *Slanguage: Dictionary of Irish Slang* (Dublin: Gill and Macmillan, 1997)

Sheedy, Larry, *That's Another Story: a Miscellany of Traveller's Tales* (Blackrock, Dublin: Irish Food Publishers, 1993)

Taub, Michael, *Jack Doyle: the Gorgeous Gael* (Dublin: The Lilliput Press, 2007; 2nd ed.)

Walsh, Patrick, *Patrick Kavanagh and* The Leader: *The Poet, the Politician and the Libel Trial* (Cork: Mercier Press, 2010)

Whelan, Barry, *Ireland's Revolutionary Diplomat: A Biography of Leopold Kerney* (Notre Dame, Indiana: Notre Dame University Press, 2019)